FARMING
WITH  E

**Promoting bio
across Europe
partridge cons**

*A summary of scientific evidence underlying the
North Sea Region Interreg PARTRIDGE project.*

https://northsearegion.eu/partridge

This publication describes how grey partridge conservation helps to address the farmland biodiversity crisis across Europe. It summarises the most relevant scientific evidence regarding grey partridge management and the biodiversity benefits associated with it. We have selected what we felt were the best and most thorough studies and papers available. We cite high-impact peer-reviewed papers wherever possible, relying on our combined experience and expertise to quote non-reviewed reports where published papers were unavailable.

Jen Brewin, Francis Buner & Julie Ewald

Partridges in a field with red dead-nettle *Lamium purpureum* Rollin Verlinde / Vilda

PARTRIDGE information panel at Oude Doorn demonstration site. NL Lars Soerink

CONTENTS

National Farmers' Union President's Foreword	7
Europe's farmland biodiversity problem	10
Interreg North Sea Region PARTRIDGE project	18
Background – the grey partridge	22
Nesting habitat – safe nest sites	32
Brood-rearing habitat – providing chick food	40
Winter cover and food	52
Predation	66
Working together for a common aim	82
References	90
Acknowledgements	100

Male partridge in a field with purple dead nettle Rollin Verlinde / Vilda

NATIONAL FARMERS' UNION PRESIDENT'S FOREWORD

Minette Batters

This book is important because it sets out an approach for successfully combining a viable farming business with increasing biodiversity and other public goods. It draws on scientific research and demonstration projects from across Europe and outlines habitat measures designed to benefit grey partridge, which is the indicator species for a healthy farmed environment.

UK farmers work hard, both to produce healthy food and deliver many essential ecosystem services including enriching habitats and improving soil and water quality. They do this while operating in a global economy, conforming to a myriad of complex regulations. Measures described in these pages such as planting wildflower mixes, managing hedgerows, maintaining grass margins and conservation headlands work because they are based on an understanding of the practical realities of food production and integrated into modern farming systems.

The fantastic work of the PARTRIDGE project demonstrates that, when farmers work together with the right kind of support and advice, they can achieve impressive conservation successes. It calls for future agri-environment schemes to go hand-in-hand with farming. Farmers need a fair contract built on trust with a proportionate approach to bureaucracy, a greater degree of flexibility and the right kind of financial support.

I hope this book will inspire farmers and policy makers across Europe and helps to shape future UK agri-environment policy which, if we get it right, has the power to achieve wildlife recovery on a much bigger scale. I know British farmers would be very proud to achieve that outcome for the benefit of us all.

MINETTE BATTERS, President of National Farmers' Union of England and Wales (NFU) and Wiltshire farmer

Harvest of cereal field Lars Soerink

EUROPE'S FARMLAND BIODIVERSITY PROBLEM

THE BIODIVERSITY CRISIS

Europe's farmland has been dramatically transformed by modernisation over the past century. These changes have increased the efficiency of food production, but they have also contributed to a widespread decline in ecosystem health, affecting water, air and soil quality as well as farmland biodiversity.

Across society, this degradation is widely recognised as a serious problem, through to the highest political levels in Europe. The targets set in the European Union's Biodiversity Strategy aim to reverse these declines, with Target 3a specifically designed to 'increase the contribution of agriculture to maintaining and enhancing biodiversity'[1].

The mid-term review on meeting these targets by 2020[2] clearly states that this will not be achieved. Therefore, tested working solutions are urgently needed to ensure that the biodiversity crisis can be halted at least by 2030.

HOW TO ACHIEVE PROGRESS

Providing real-world examples that reverse the ongoing decline of farmland biodiversity over large areas, and in different countries and regions, is crucial to addressing the farmland biodiversity crisis across Europe. People typically only believe what they see working with their own eyes, whether they are farmers, hunters, conservationists, local authorities, policy makers or governments.

The NSR Interreg PARTRIDGE project (referred to as PARTRIDGE throughout this booklet) was initiated to specifically fill this gap, providing a way forward to address the farmland biodiversity crisis across Europe. This project aims to demonstrate how farmland biodiversity can be reversed at 10 real-life demonstration sites, based on scientific grey partridge conservation knowledge.

WHY THE GREY PARTRIDGE?

The grey partridge is one of the most rapidly declining farmland birds in Europe - its numbers have declined by more than 90% since the 1970s[3]. It has also been the subject of thorough research, so we have a more detailed picture of what is driving the decline in grey partridge numbers than for many other species sharing the same farmland ecosystem.

Labelled a 'barometer of the countryside'[4], the grey partridge is an ideal indicator of arable farmland ecosystem health: where partridges thrive, other farmland wildlife also thrives.

WHY THE PARTRIDGE PROJECT?

Several conservation projects across Europe, either at a small scale on single farms or across groups of farms, have shown that well-designed conservation measures are effective in helping grey partridges. Research and practical conservation initiatives from various parts of Europe show that where partridge conservation measures are introduced, a wide range of other farmland species benefit.

PARTRIDGE pulls together these management elements into a practical and effective conservation package that works alongside profitable farming, as long as those who implement the necessary measures are adequately compensated for their efforts.

Across Europe financial support is provided by Agri-Environment (AE) schemes. These AE schemes are the key policy instrument of the EU's Common Agricultural Policy (CAP), aiming to reverse the decline of farmland biodiversity by incorporating wildlife-friendly management into farming businesses[5].

Besides farmers, other rural stakeholders also have a part to play in conserving grey partridges and other farmland biodiversity. PARTRIDGE demonstrates the feasibility of this in an innovative way, regardless of state borders.

THE PARTRIDGE PROJECT BRINGS TOGETHER THE KNOWLEDGE AND UNDERSTANDING FROM INITIATIVES ACROSS EUROPE, INTO ONE PRACTICAL PACKAGE FOR FARMLAND WILDLIFE RECOVERY BASED ON GREY PARTRIDGE CONSERVATION

2000

WHY THIS BOOKLET?

This booklet provides an overview of the grey partridge conservation research from across Europe applied within PARTRIDGE. It briefly explains grey partridge biology, the key management measures needed for this species' survival and the benefits of grey partridge conservation for farmland wildlife in general.

It is only through applying well-tested conservation approaches across regions and countries, and by developing them further, that we will ensure the recovery of farmland biodiversity today and a healthy future for us all.

FUTURE

PARTRIDGE partners at Ramskapelle demonstration site, Belgium Willem van Colen

INTERREG NORTH SEA REGION PARTRIDGE PROJECT

The PARTRIDGE project is an international collaboration between 13 European partners from within the North Sea Region. Together, we manage ten 500-hectare demonstration sites (two each in England, Scotland, the Netherlands, Belgium and Germany), where the project has established and improved conservation measures developed for grey partridges, but which can benefit many species.

PARTRIDGE aims for a 30% increase in farmland biodiversity by 2023 in all of its demonstration sites, measuring farmland wildlife indicators such as grey partridge, breeding songbird and brown hare numbers. These support the targets in the EU's Biodiversity Strategy for agricultural land.

We have tailored our approach to the needs of each country, to demonstrate how to successfully increase farmland biodiversity across the EU. We actively promote our solutions among a wide range of relevant stakeholder groups, and seek to influence agri-environmental policy, especially by holding farm walk events tailored to those different groups at our demonstration areas. Our Swedish and Danish partners actively promote our solutions in their respective countries, although we have no demonstration sites there.

Our approach can be incorporated into standard farming practices regardless of region or country, which is key to persuading governments to support these methods through national AE schemes or equivalent alternatives that may be available in the future.

United Kingdom
Game & Wildlife Conservation Trust - *Lead partner*

Netherlands
BirdLife Netherlands - *Co-ordinating partner*

Stichting Landschapsbeheer Zeeland

Brabants Landschap

Stichting Het Zeeuwse Landschap

Germany
Georg-August-Universität, Abt. Naturschutzbiologie

Belgium
Flemish Land Agency (VLM) - *Co-ordinating partner*

Research Institute for Nature and Forest (INBO)

Inagro

Boerennatuur Vlaanderen

Flemish Hunters Association (HVV)

Denmark
Danish Hunters Association

Sweden
Odling I Balans

Grey partridge pair Markus Jenny

BACKGROUND – THE GREY PARTRIDGE

LIFE CYCLE

Grey partridges are ground-dwelling birds that are site-faithful, spending their life within a few kilometres of where they hatch. They roost and nest on the ground and have the largest average clutch size of all birds (15 eggs in north-west Europe). If the first clutch is lost, grey partridges will make a second attempt at breeding with a replacement clutch, which contains fewer eggs. First clutches tend to hatch from the middle of June and replacement ones up until early August.

When they hatch, the chicks are mobile almost immediately and the adults move the chicks off the nest within a few hours to suitable areas nearby where they can find food. Chicks forage on the ground in tall but relatively open farmland vegetation, eating mainly insects and their larvae for the first two weeks. Their diet then changes to include seeds, grains and green leaves of grasses, cereals and flowering plants[6-9].

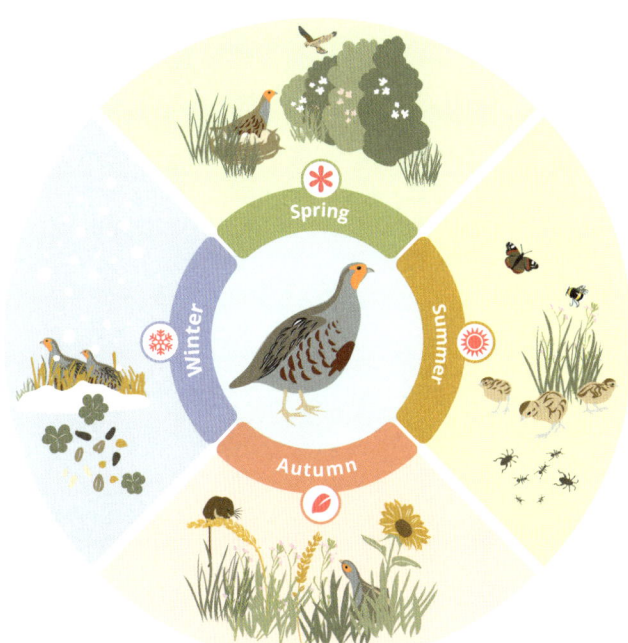

Figure 1 In this guide we describe the habitat measures that provide resources for the partridge's life cycle throughout the year.

There are pinchpoints for grey partridge survival in every season. Our habitat measures are aimed at making improvements to address each of these bottlenecks.

The chicks' early reliance on a high-protein diet made up mainly of insects has important implications, both for understanding the needs of the grey partridge and for designing conservation strategies to support them. Chicks become capable of flight at around 10-15 days. The family group, sometimes joined by other adults, stays together in a covey through the summer and winter before breaking up. The young then form pairs with individuals from neighbouring coveys for the next breeding season. Grey partridge pairs stay together throughout the year.

PARTRIDGE DECLINES

Across Europe over the past 150 years, grey partridge abundance shows three distinct trends (as shown in Figure 2). The general pattern is of stable high numbers in the late 1800s to 1950s/60s, then a sharp decline, followed by an ongoing more gradual decline[10-14].

These trends coincide with changes in farming methods. In the late 1800s to mid-1900s, farming methods provided good habitat for partridges and numbers were high.

The 1950s-1960s saw the widespread introduction of herbicides. This affected grey partridges and other farmland species by disrupting the food chain, removing weeds (arable flora) which are the host plants for insects that partridge chicks depend upon for food (Figure 3)[15-18].

Some of the early insecticides whose usage also became common around this time were directly toxic to partridges[19]. More recently, although most insecticide treatments applied to fields are not directly toxic to farmland birds[20], they still affect grey partridges - and other insect-eating farmland birds - by reducing the abundance of insects important in chick diet[18,21].

Figure 2 Changes in partridge abundance through time across Europe. Numbers have generally followed three phases: high and stable numbers historically, followed by a steep decline from around the early 1950s to the 1990s and a continuing, more gradual decline thereafter. These trends mainly reflect changes in agricultural practice.

PARTRIDGE CHICKS ARE COMPLETELY DEPENDENT ON INSECT FOOD DURING THEIR FIRST TWO WEEKS OF LIFE

Figure 3 Grey partridge chicks rely on insects during their first two weeks of life. This food supply can be disrupted directly by the use of insecticides, which kill the insects. Or, indirectly by the use of herbicides, which kill the plants that support the chicks' insect food.

KEY FACTORS IMPLICATED IN GREY PARTRIDGE DECLINES

Extensive research across Europe in the second half of the 20th century has helped us understand grey partridge declines in more detail. Across the continent, the three main reasons are:

- Loss of insects from cropped fields because of herbicide and insecticide use.
    - This lack of food led to smaller broods, i.e. fewer surviving young per nesting female[11,22,23].
- Loss of nesting habitat because hedgerows and grass banks were removed, and fields combined.
    - This led to fewer successful breeding pairs in spring[24-26].
- Increased predation, especially by generalist predators such as the red fox, because of land use changes, a reduction in legal predator control and a change in the behaviour of hunters[27].
    - This led to higher losses, particularly of nesting females[28,29].

This trio of causes was first proposed by the British farmland ecologist Dr Dick Potts in the 1970s as the 'three-legged stool'[8]. His theory, now widely accepted, was based on his own scientific studies in the UK[23], influenced by other studies of grey partridge ecology[6-9], and is supported by more recent research[30-33]. Modern farming methods either affect all three legs of the stool or affect one so much that 'the whole stool becomes unsteady'.

Further research suggests a fourth element: poor survival during the late-winter period. It is thought to be driven by predation and worsened by the lack of suitable winter cover and food resources[20,31,34,35].

The collapse of the three-legged stool has affected both partridge numbers and the wildlife that thrives alongside them. Reinstating the supporting legs can provide a stable foundation for farmland biodiversity. Farmland conservation based on this model has been shown to successfully increase both partridge numbers[36,37] and farmland biodiversity as a whole[38-41], by providing nesting habitat, brood-rearing habitat, winter cover and food, and by managing predation.

These topics are examined individually in the following chapters.

Conservation headland, Sussex, England Peter Thompson

Partridge female with chicks David Mason

NESTING HABITAT – SAFE NEST SITES

Key point
Partridges need plenty of high-quality nesting habitat.

Provided by
Permanent and semi-permanent vegetation features such as wildflower plots, hedgerows, grass margins and beetle banks.

Grey partridges nest on the ground. The preferred nest site is in unmown tussocky grasses with old vegetation, typically found along hedgerows, ditches, dikes or grassy field margins that have plenty of dead grass from the previous year[24,42]. Nests can also be found in the crops themselves, especially cereals[43].

In recent years AE schemes have introduced some habitats that can replace or augment the more traditional grassy nesting habitats that are now scarce in modern farmland. These include wildflower plots[44,45], beetle banks that provide suitable nesting cover in the middle of large arable fields and field corners or fallow land[8].

THE EVIDENCE for partridges

Although partridges prefer to nest in vegetation with unmown tussocky grasses, actual nesting sites vary across Europe depending on the available habitat. For example, in the UK 65% of partridge nests are found in field margins, including the base of hedgerows, grassy banks or uncut margins[24,46]. In Germany nearly 95% of grey partridge nests were found in similar permanent vegetation, with a quarter in wildflower blocks specifically designed to provide nesting and foraging habitat in the breeding season[44]. Conversely, in north-central France, 65% of grey partridge nests were found in cereal crops, with only 13% in linear features like hedges[43].

This indicates that the availability of habitat types influences grey partridge nest-site selection.

In PARTRIDGE, the quality and quantity of nesting habitats on demonstration sites are increased both through changes in management of existing habitats and provision of new habitats. This includes implementing hedgerow management, adding in new grass margins and beetle banks, and ensuring grass margins are not mown before chicks can fly. The mowing date will differ slightly between regions, for example, in Germany it is recommended not to mow before 15 August. Where appropriate we are involving agencies such as water boards in Flanders (Belgium) to adjust their mowing regimes and ensure nests are not destroyed during the breeding season.

Partridge breeding density is closely associated with the amount of available nesting cover: where there is more high-quality cover, there are more partridges, and increasing the amount available can increase partridge breeding densities[10,25,33,43,47].

Five main habitats are known to provide nesting cover across farmland: hedgerows, grass margins and ditches, wildflower plots, beetle banks and cereal crops.

For hedgerows, grass margins and ditches to provide optimal nesting cover, management is key. For example, in the spring these features should retain enough dead grass or similar vegetation from the previous year to provide cover for a female grey partridge sitting on a nest[8,9,24]. This also means that they need to remain uncut during the nesting season to avoid destroying the nest and killing the sitting female. Hedges should be cut in rotation (up to every three years), to allow a dense base to develop[24].

Wildflower plots can provide ideal nesting sites because of their open structure at ground level, combined with vegetation that provides suitable cover and camouflage. In Switzerland and Germany, partridges preferred to nest and spend time in or near wildflower plots[44,45].

It is essential not to mow these areas when females are incubating or when chicks are very young (May-August). Management of wildflower plots is discussed further on pages 42-44.

Several successful UK partridge recovery projects have used beetle banks to provide additional nesting habitat[48-50]. This is because they are dry and disconnected from the edges of the field, which may reduce predation[51]. Beetle banks are quicker and easier to establish than a traditional hedgerow.

However, linear nesting habitats like beetle banks or those along field boundaries are usually not appropriate in areas without lethal predator management, because they can act as corridors to concentrate predators and prey, and lead to more predation rather than less[43,44].

For other species

Hedgerows are important habitats for farmland invertebrates[52,53], being able to support more than 1,500 different invertebrate species from 70 families. Hawthorn alone has 209 species associated with it[54]. Many butterflies such as small tortoiseshell, red admiral, gatekeeper, orange tip, ringlet, and several whites are commonly found alongside farmland hedgerows[55].

Many declining farmland bird species rely on hedgerows as nesting habitats, for instance yellowhammer, whitethroat, linnet, and turtle dove[56].

Beetle banks were designed to provide overwintering sites for beneficial insects[57], with higher numbers in fields with beetle banks[58] than in those without. Invertebrates such as predatory ground beetles use tussocky grasses to shelter overwinter, and thousands can be found per square metre on a beetle bank[59,60]. These can reduce the number of pest insects, for example aphids, in the nearby crop in spring and summer[58].

Beetle banks are also a haven for other farmland wildlife. Together with grass margins and wildflower plots, they provide ideal nest sites for small mammals such as harvest mouse[61,62], common vole[63], and brown hare[64].

Beetle banks are raised banks (0.5m high by 3m wide) that are sown with a mix of tussocky grasses, typically dividing a field in two but not connecting to the field edges.

Beetle banks were invented in the UK in the early 1990s where, based on research, they made it into the English AE scheme in the mid-1990s, and Scottish and Welsh schemes shortly thereafter.

PARTRIDGE introduced beetle banks to the Netherlands in 2017, Belgium in 2018, and Germany in 2019. They were adopted into AE schemes in the Netherlands in 2018 as a direct result of the PARTRIDGE project. PARTRIDGE aims to introduce beetle banks into the AE schemes of all North Sea member states.

Harvest mouse David Kjaer

37

PARTRIDGE flower block at Diemarden demonstration site, Germany Eckhard Gottschalk

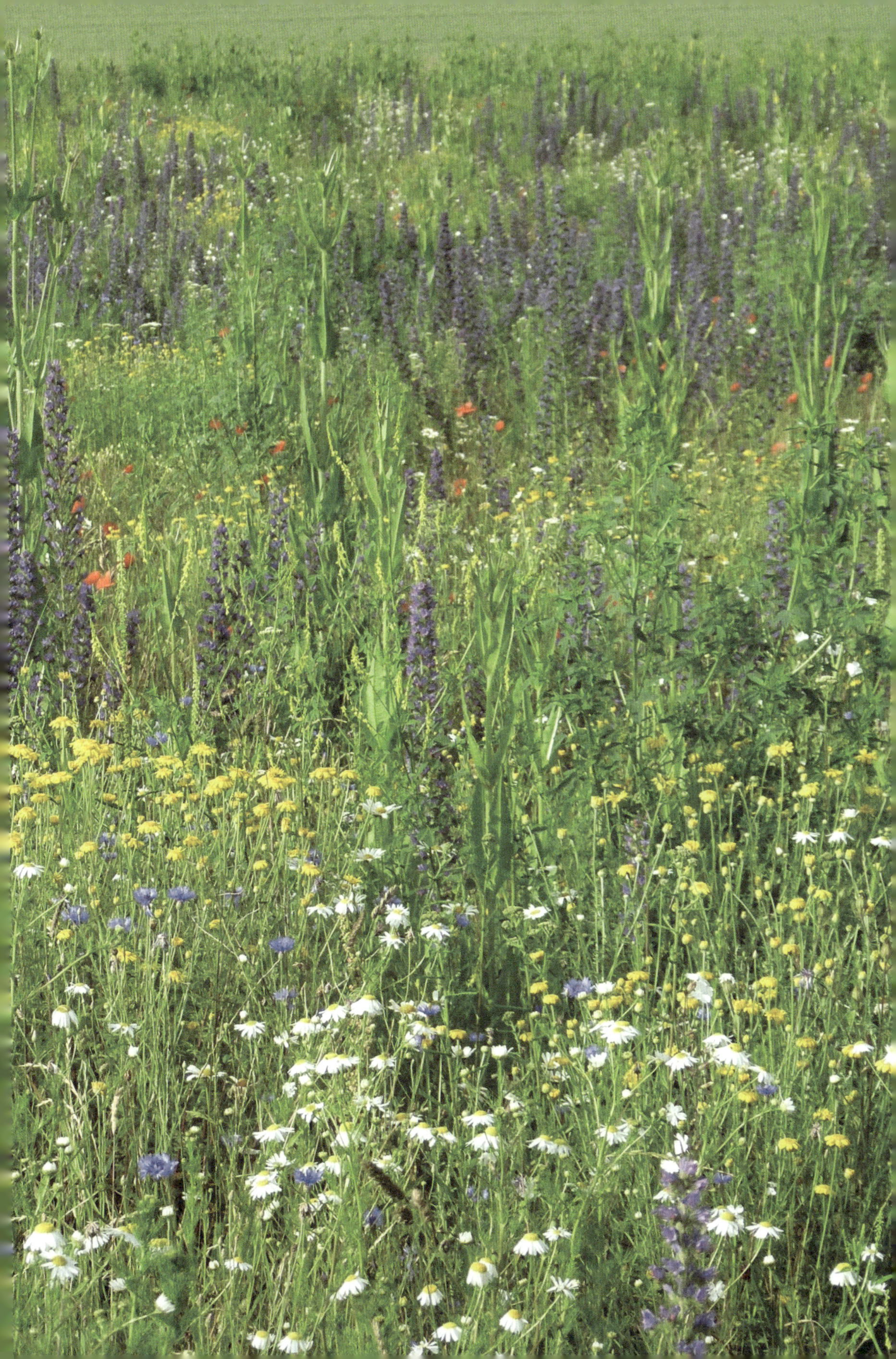

BROOD-REARING HABITAT – PROVIDING CHICK FOOD

Key point
Partridge chicks need insect-rich foraging habitat, near to where they hatch, to survive the first few weeks of life.

Provided by
Wildflower plots, conservation headlands, annual arable margins.

In the first two weeks of life, grey partridge chicks eat mainly insects[16]. This high-protein diet is very important for chick growth and, if other factors are favourable, the more insect-food there is, the better chicks will survive.

Guided by their parents, partridge chicks forage for insects within an area of 4-10 hectares, depending on how much habitat providing chick food is available near the nest[45].

It is critical for partridge conservation to provide a rich and accessible supply of insects close to the nest. It is commonly believed that chick mortality increases if the family group (covey) must travel some distance to find food, as they are more vulnerable to predation and bad weather conditions.

THE PARTRIDGE PROJECT USES WILDFLOWER PLOTS TO PROVIDE INSECT-RICH FORAGING HABITAT

THE EVIDENCE for partridges

The insects that grey partridge chicks eat live on plants within crops, or on the crops themselves[18]. These plants are known as arable flora or, more commonly, weeds. Insect declines across the globe have recently received great attention[65]. Removing either weeds with herbicides[8,66] or insects with insecticides[67] destroys the chicks' food supply (see Figure 3, page 27).

In the UK, before the introduction of herbicides, grey partridge chick survival averaged 49%. This dropped to 32% once they were widely used[11].

Decreased chick survival was then the main driver of the grey partridge decline: not enough chicks were making it to adulthood, so numbers were falling. Increased insecticide use added to the problem, with grey partridge chick survival a third lower in areas of widespread insecticide use than in areas with little or no use[22]. This seminal work from the UK has been replicated most recently in Poland, where increases in pesticide use are correlated with declining chick survival rates[167].

Therefore, areas that receive no or only selective pesticide treatments during the summer can provide a haven for chicks. On modern farms these are provided by wildflower plots, conservation headlands (see page 45), or other forms of open, insect-rich vegetation[15,68].

It is essential that brood-rearing habitats provided for grey partridge chicks are not treated with summer insecticides. The accepted management of weeds varies, with some habitats receiving no herbicide. Selective herbicides that remove only pernicious weeds but do not harm the plant species that support insects can be used where needed.

The structure of the vegetation in these areas is also very important. There needs to be a canopy for protection from aerial predators such as raptors and corvids, but the underlying structure needs to be more open to allow chicks to move freely through the habitat[15,68].

The seed mixes used in wildflower plots in PARTRIDGE contain various flowers and other plant species chosen for their ability to support insects[69,70], produce seeds for adult birds[71-74] and give overhead protection. Four times as many insects have been found in wildflower strips as in conventional wheat fields[75,76]. Adding wildflower plots to the landscape (typically up to 1 hectare but sometimes larger) stabilised the previously declining grey partridge numbers across a large study area in Germany[44]. In one area where these wildflower plots covered 7% of farmland, grey partridge numbers increased 10-fold[44].

In the UK, wildflower plots have been associated with larger grey partridge broods, more young per adult and improved grey partridge survival in winter[77]. In Switzerland, reintroduced grey partridges chose to settle in areas with the most wildflower strips and hedges[45].

Wildflower plots are the key habitat measure recommended by PARTRIDGE. PARTRIDGE uses blocks or wide strips (at least 20 metres wide) sown with a mix of different flower species to provide good habitat for partridges.

Much consideration has gone into developing mixes that suit the project's varying local conditions, ensuring suitable nesting, foraging and winter habitat all year round at all the demonstration sites.

They are managed in a rotation to achieve this. Alternate halves of each plot are re-established each year in spring or autumn (depending on local conditions), and the differently aged vegetation on the two halves provides habitat variety. Having more variety in the structure and composition of the mixes results in higher biodiversity overall.

The key plants used are sunflower, mustard, kale, chicory, perennial rye, lucerne (alfalfa), sweet clover and teasel. Various other species are added to the mix at different sites to increase diversity and suitability for farmland biodiversity.

Flower power

In PARTRIDGE, the mixes were developed taking into consideration seed prices, to ensure that the cost of the mix was acceptable to farmers, while also including as many native species as possible. The seeds of native species are usually more expensive, so although an entirely native mix would be desirable, a compromise was needed for PARTRIDGE.

The literature describing wildflower plots varies in how they are named. Sometimes they are referred to as wildflower mixes, in other cases as wild bird seed mixes. In this document, we use wildflower mix when referring to seed mixes, and wildflower plot when referring to the area once it is sown. Where size, shape or species composition is important, we highlight that. Where we refer to a paper that mentions such plots, we use the same terminology as the paper.

PARTRIDGE flower block at Diemarden demonstration site, D, Eckhard Gottschalk

Conservation headlands are currently supported by AE schemes in the UK and Switzerland. They are strips around the edge of cereal fields, usually 6-12 metres wide, which are part of the crop but managed with no or only selective pesticides during the summer. They may also be sown at lower densities and may have a lower nitrogen input. This allows arable plants (weeds) to grow, and supports the insects that grey partridge chicks need[15,78].

More than twice as many insects have been found in conservation headlands compared with headlands sprayed as normal[15]. This more plentiful food supply can improve chick survival[15,68,78–80].

Annual arable margins, also called cultivated margins and including floristically-enhanced margins, are uncropped strips around fields that are renewed each year. They are usually 3-6 metres wide and aim to provide habitat for arable plants, in particular those that are rare or endangered. In the case of cultivated uncropped margins, they are ploughed and left unsown to allow natural regeneration of weeds from the seeds in the soil, while sown/floristically-enhanced arable margins are sown with native arable flora.

They are expected to give good foraging habitat for partridge chicks and may act as a substitute for, or addition to, conservation headlands because they benefit chick-food insects[81–83]. Sown weed strips (floristically-enhanced margins) are very attractive to insects[82].

The conservation value of field margins sown with a seed mix compared with naturally regenerated strips will vary greatly, depending on the soil type, the seeds present in the soil and the management approach. Arable margins are also supported by AE schemes in several European countries.

In PARTRIDGE we provide brood-rearing habitat mainly using wildflower plots and arable margins – both cultivated and sown. The key is to provide a lightly managed vegetation, rich in floral resources, that will support the necessary chick-food insects, with an open structure to allow chicks to forage.

Roe deer in Swiss wildflower plot Markus Jenny

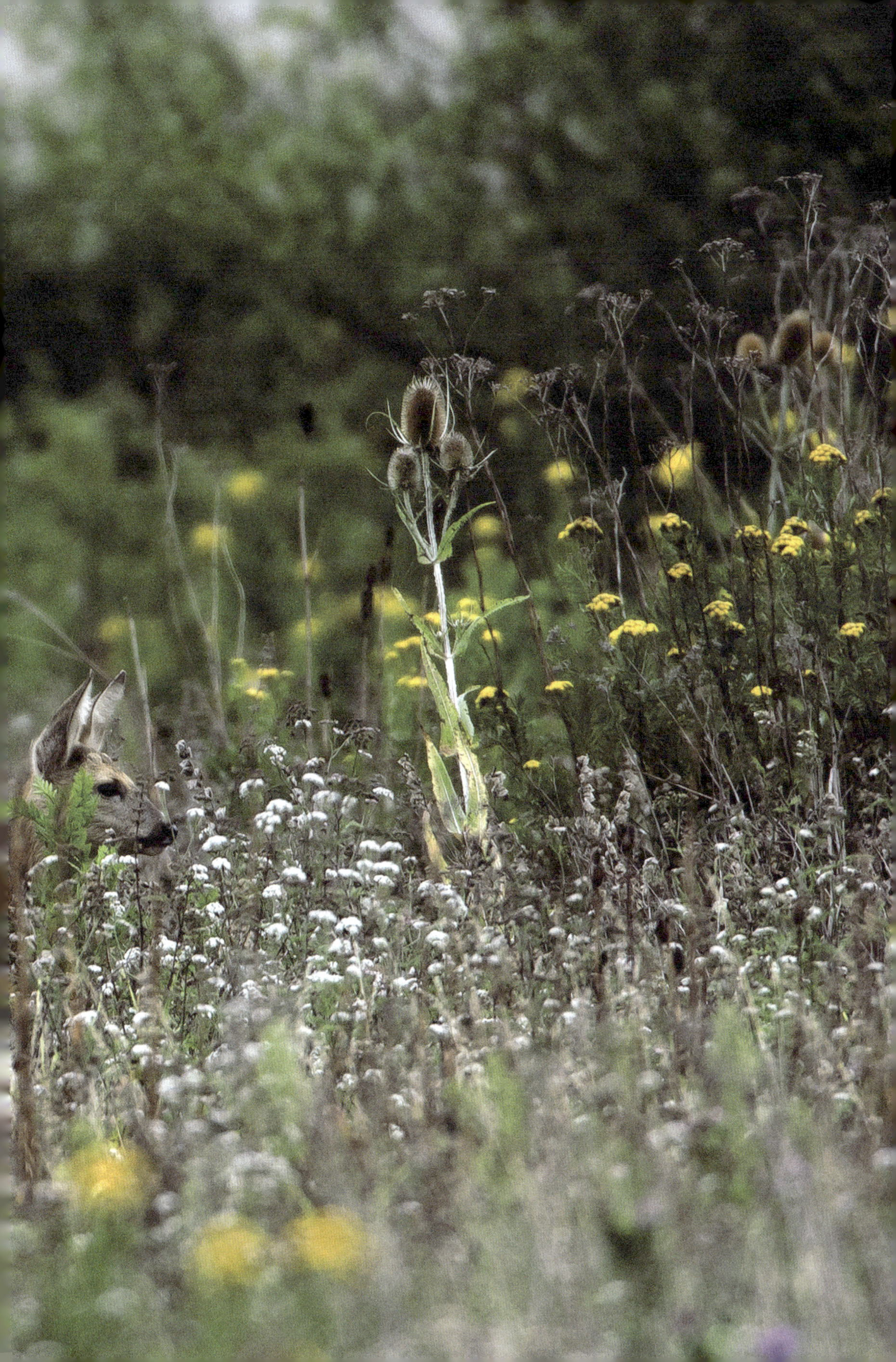

For other species

Wildflower plots provide good habitat for a variety of species, many of which are found in higher numbers than in adjacent conventional crops[84]. These include the common vole[85,86], a range of farmland birds[87] such as skylark[88], corn bunting[89], kestrel[86], and long-eared owl[86]. Many insects and spiders[90,91] can also benefit, including ground beetles[92], hoverflies[93], butterflies and moths[74,82], and wild bees[74,82]. Wildflower plots also contain high numbers of beneficial predatory insects, which can help control pest outbreaks in nearby crops[94,95].

Although conservation headlands were originally designed to aid grey partridge numbers, they are also beneficial for other species. Many invertebrates including butterflies are more abundant in these areas[15,96,97]. More food is available for butterflies in conservation headlands, so feeding is more efficient and butterflies are able to spend more time resting and interacting with each other[98]. The increased number of flowers[39] in conservation headlands attracts hoverflies, whose larvae eat crop pests such as aphids[99]. Conservation headlands also provide ideal habitat for small mammals such as wood mice, who actively seek out these areas[100].

Cultivated arable margins and extensively managed cereals were developed to aid arable flora. Cultivated arable margins were deemed to have the potential to conserve up to 40 species of rare arable flora[101] and a system of cereal fields managed with little or no agricultural chemicals ('extensively' managed) has been used to create mini-nature reserves for arable flora across Germany in the '100 Fields for Diversity' programme[102].

In addition to arable flora, more spiders and ground beetles are found in cultivated arable margins compared with conventionally cropped margins in spring[81,103], and they are known to be beneficial to other farmland birds such as corn bunting[89,104].

Another role that wildflower plots, conservation headlands and other AE scheme measures can fulfil is that of a buffer for agricultural chemicals. Where there are areas of unsprayed vegetation such as conservation headlands or wildflower plots at the edge of fields, there is less pesticide drift onto adjacent hedgerows, ditches and bodies of water. This reduces the effects of pesticides on insect populations in field boundary features[105,106] and on nearby aquatic life[107].

Bumblebee *Bombus pratorum* on marsh thistle *Cirsium palustre* Peter Thompson

Partridge in winter cover Dick Forsman / Agami

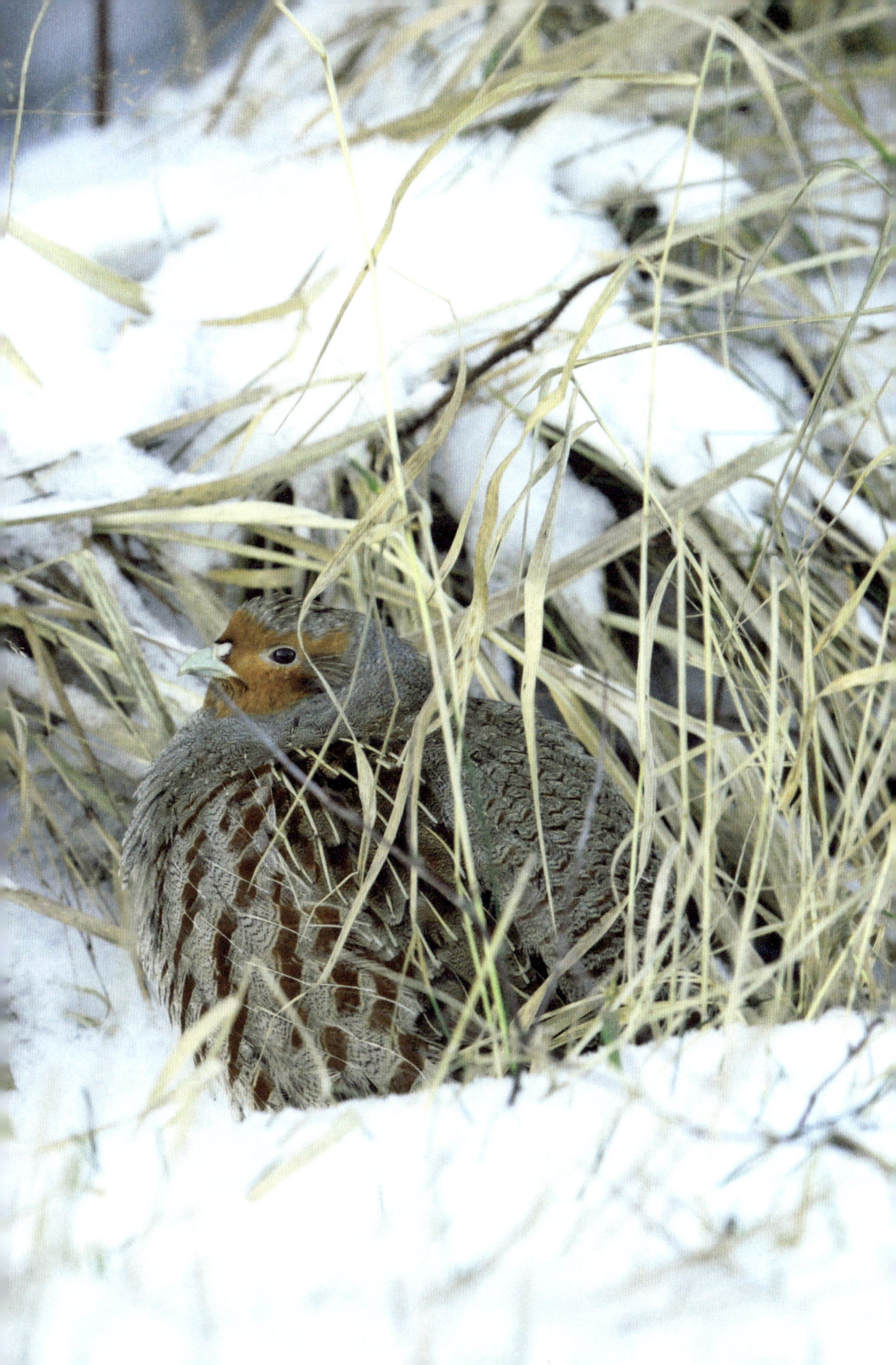

WINTER COVER AND FOOD

Key point
Winter survival is improved by cover and food.

Provided by
Wildflower mixes, winter stubbles, supplementary feeding.

Measures to improve grey partridge winter survival are an important part of partridge conservation packages. These consist of providing winter cover, which gives protection from severe weather and predators[108,109].

Lack of food over winter can also be a problem because seeds are scarce on modern farmland in winter[110], particularly during the period known as the 'hungry gap', which runs from January to early May in north-western Europe[111].

Wildflower plots sown for nesting and brood-rearing can also provide seed resources and cover in winter for grey partridges and other farmland wildlife[34]. This requires careful selection of the species included in these mixes because they need to hold seeds until early spring.

Although grey partridge adults eat mainly leaves and other plant matter in winter[112], additional feeding with grain is often used to supplement their natural food.

For some countries in north-west Europe, where comparatively few plant species bear seeds into early spring, it may be difficult to grow plants that provide seed into mid-February. In these cases, supplementary feeding may be even more important.

The thinking on supplementary feeding is two-fold: firstly it could reduce foraging time and hence predation risk[108], and secondly high-energy food, such as seeds, may lead to better breeding condition[113].

THE EVIDENCE for partridges

A review of scientific evidence from across Europe found that winter survival of females was a key factor in population growth[29,35]. Because grey partridges stay in the same area all year round, they must find enough food and cover from predators during winter.

Radio-tracking studies carried out during the winter months in Germany and Switzerland have shown that grey partridges spend most of their time in the middle of arable fields, in particular cereal fields, stubbles and oilseed rape[44,45]. During this time, they feed mainly on the shoots of short winter crops, while taller vegetation provides cover from predators.

Winter stubbles

Winter stubbles are crop stalks left in the ground over winter. Winter stubbles, especially weedy ones or those sown with a structurally open cover crop, provide a valuable resource for partridges and other seed-eating farmland birds[110,114]. In the past, cereals were sown with ley crops (grass/legumes), resulting in undersown green stubbles post-harvest. This practice had benefits for sawfly larvae – important chick-food insects – but has largely been abandoned[4].

The diet of grey partridges feeding in stubble fields is more varied than those feeding in winter-sown cereal fields or oilseed rape, with more grain and seeds compared with mostly leaves[112]. Although a predominantly leaf-based diet is sufficient for grey partridges, it is generally thought that seeds provide a more nutritious diet[8].

Stubble fields also provide cover for grey partridges during the winter, another important factor in their overwinter survival[108]. Unfortunately, winter stubbles are now uncommon on farmland, following changes in cropping and management of cereal fields[115]. Where they still exist, they contain lower seed resources owing to intensive management of the crop preceding the stubble, as well as more efficient harvesting techniques[116].

Cover

Cover is needed to help partridges avoid predation in winter. Grey partridge winter losses across Europe range from 30-81% of autumn partridge numbers[31,34,117,118], with particularly high losses seen in late winter and early spring[34,108]. Grey partridges are five times more likely to experience predation in winter on days with snow cover than on snow-free days[44]. This is assumed to be because they are much easier for predators to spot when they lose the protection provided by their camouflage.

Supplementary feeding

Seed food for farmland birds can be scarce during the hungry gap in late winter[111]. Providing supplementary seed food during winter has become commonplace on shooting estates across Europe, where it is thought to help maintain partridges in good condition into the breeding season. The effect of this has not been scientifically tested for grey partridges, but it is known to help another gamebird, the pheasant, gain better body condition during the breeding period[119,120].

Supplementary feeding may also decrease foraging time, and therefore reduce vulnerability to predation. During times of high snow cover, supplementary feeding may also reduce winter mortality, however, neither of these aspects have been scientifically tested. It is known that partridges utilise feeders and that some areas with extensive winter feeding in France have high partridge densities[121].

For other species

Breeding populations of many farmland birds are in decline, and the reduced amount of seed available to them in modern farming systems contributes to this[72,115]. Stubble fields, particularly weedy ones, may provide a good source of grain and weed seeds in early winter[122], and many species of farmland birds are known to feed in them, including skylark, linnet, yellowhammer and reed bunting as well as grey partridge[123]. A loss of weedy stubble fields is one of the factors contributing to their decline[115].

A comparison of seed-bearing crops with conventional crops across 192 farmland sites in the UK found that overall, winter bird densities were more than 12 times higher on these plots. When the analysis was confined to the 'most preferred' of those seed crops, this rose to 50 times higher[73]. This is just one of many studies that show the value of seed-bearing crops in winter to many farmland bird species[72].

In Scottish plots sown with mixes consisting of kale, triticale, mustard and quinoa, up to 100 times as many songbirds per hectare were recorded during the winter compared with set-aside, stubble or conventional crops. The plots in this study attracted 50% more bird species than set aside or cereal stubble, and 91% more species than conventional crops, including linnet, reed bunting, tree sparrow and song thrush[71]. Researchers in the Netherlands found a much higher density of farmland birds within winter food plots than on the farmland nearby[124].

Overwintering arthropods were found in higher densities in sown wildflower strips in Switzerland than in arable fields[125]. In the UK, small mammals (mainly wood mouse) have been shown to use wild bird cover crops more than conventional cereals in the winter[126]. In Switzerland kestrels and long-eared owls benefit from this, with wild bird cover being their preferred hunting habitat over winter due to an increased density of field voles[86].

Providing extra seed for birds during winter can help increase their winter survival and breeding condition[127]. In the UK, when grain feeders were provided for gamebirds in winter, they were also visited by many other species including dunnock, blackbird and yellowhammer[128].

At one site in the UK, the years with no winter feeding had fewer seed-eating songbirds, particularly in late winter[129–131]. In this study, songbirds accounted for 38% of visits to the feeder. Thanks to this research, supplementary feeding in late winter is now supported by AE schemes in England. At the Allerton Project study area at Loddington, the abundance of songbirds decreased after winter feeding was stopped[131].

THE PARTRIDGE PROJECT ADOPTS MEASURES TO IMPROVE SURVIVAL OF FARMLAND BIRDS IN WINTER

Greenfinch and bramblings feeding in PARTRIDGE flower block at Burgh Sluis demonstration site, NL Jannie Timmer

The PARTRIDGE flower plots provide suitable cover and food for partridges and other farmland birds at least through early winter as they include sunflowers, teasel and chicory. The hollow stems of sunflowers and teasel make ideal overwintering or nesting sites for wild solitary bees and other insects. The flower plots also attract small mammals that are food for wintering raptors and owls. Providing supplementary winter food helps partridges and other farmland birds to bridge the hungry gap during winter months.

Partridge covey at feeder Chris Knights

Winter aspect of PARTRIDGE autumn-sown mix at Diemarden demonstration site, Germany. Eckhard Gottschalk

WHAT DOES THE IDEAL PARTRIDGE LANDSCAPE LOOK LIKE?

There is no strict 'correct' way to arrange partridge-friendly habitats in the landscape, although there are some guiding principles. The objective is to provide all necessary habitat requirements summarised in this booklet (nesting, brood-rearing and winter cover) in the territory of a grey partridge pair.

Ideally brood-rearing cover, which could be a first-year PARTRIDGE wildflower plot, arable margin or conservation headland, should be next to nesting cover, provided by either a hedge, unmown grass margin or beetle bank. A sterile or bare strip nearby allows chicks to dry in the sun after a summer rain shower and search for insects. The illustration on the following page shows an idealistic layout, that can be applied with local adjustments at any farmland biodiversity recovery project across Europe[44,45,80,121,130,132].

HOW MUCH SUITABLE HABITAT DO WE NEED?

Early work from Switzerland on the area of land needed to maintain biodiversity on farmland concluded that between 12% and 15% needed to be managed for conservation to maintain the existing biodiversity on lowland farmland[133,134]. The EU set targets for 5% of arable land to be used for ecological focus areas, with little consideration for the quality of this area[135].

PARTRIDGE recommends managing a minimum of 7% of the total arable area for grey partridges, made up of high-quality habitat distributed as evenly across the project area as possible. This figure is based on several scientific studies examining the effect that increased nesting and brood-rearing cover may have on partridge chick survival[8,15,24,25], as well as the effect of non-cropped areas[136], natural areas, or 'Ecological Compensation Areas' on farmland birds or biodiversity more broadly[138].

HOW BIG DOES THE PROJECT AREA NEED TO BE?

For grey partridge conservation projects, the area can vary from as little as 400 hectares[139] (the minimum recommendation), to as large as 100,000 hectares[44]. PARTRIDGE demonstration sites are the result of a compromise between the desirable and the feasible. Therefore, the project partners decided on an area of 500 hectares for each demonstration site.

Depending on the country, this can mean that up to 30 neighbouring farmers must cooperate to implement 7% high-quality wildlife habitat across the 500-hectare demonstration area. This is a huge challenge in itself. It can only be achieved by the collaboration and involvement of many different stakeholders including farmers, hunters, local, regional and national conservation organisations, volunteers from the local communities, farm advisors, scientists and government bodies.

Ditch

Flower-rich tussocky grass margin *3 metres*

Arable crop *100-200 metres*

PARTRIDGE wildflower plot *min. 20 metres*

Sterile strip *1 metre*

Figure 4 An idealised arrangement of PARTRIDGE conservation measures for farmland biodiversity recovery projects in Europe. When applied together, they provide for the needs of grey partridges all year round and allow farmland wildlife generally to recover.

Beetle bank
3 metres

Conservation headland
min. 4 metres

Arable crop
100-200 metres

PARTRIDGE wildflower plot
min. 20 metres

Flower-rich tussocky grass margin *3 metres*

Hedgerow

Partridge covey in flight Jari Peltomäki / Agami

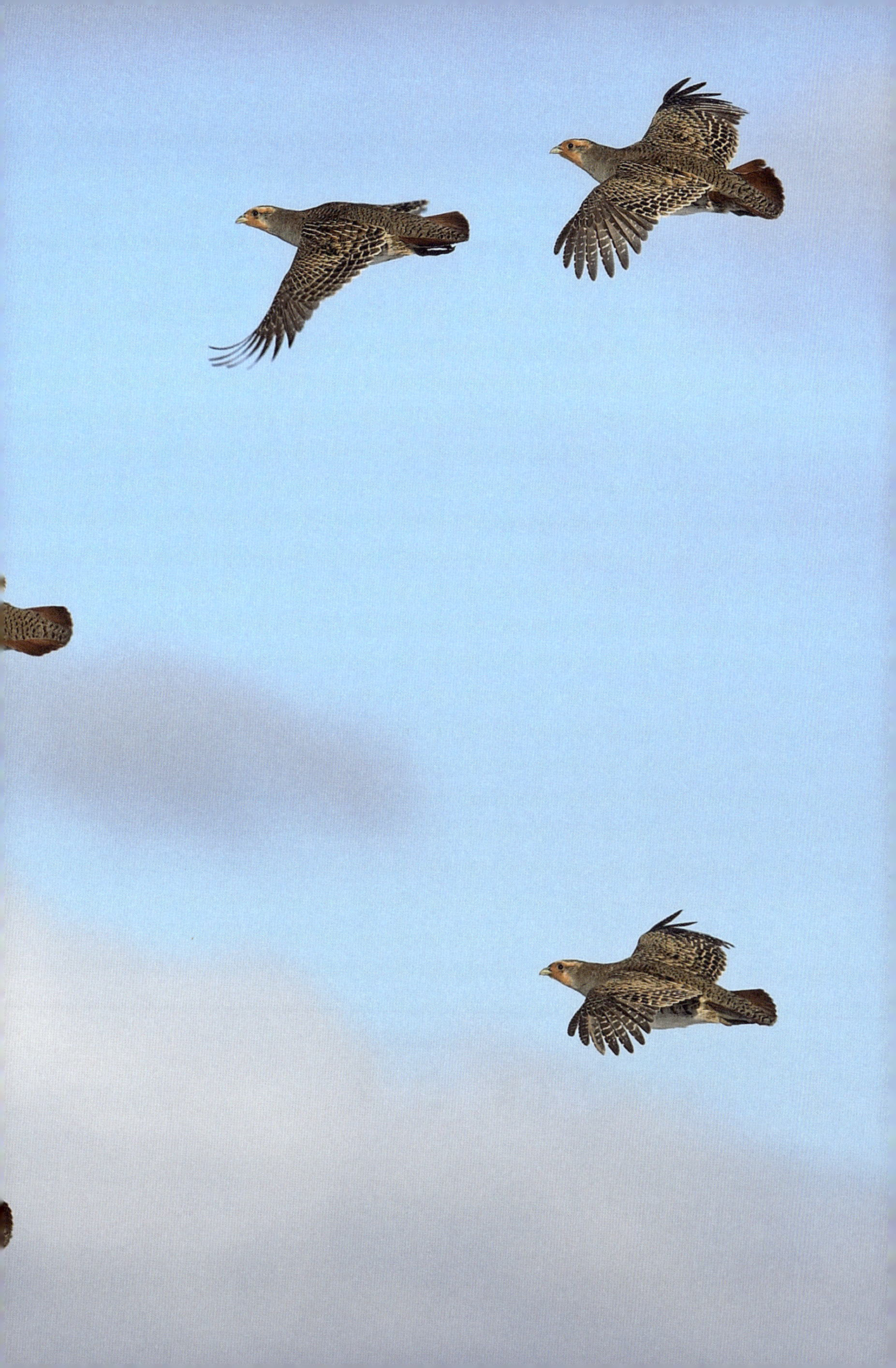

PREDATION

Key point
Partridge abundance is heavily affected by predation; reducing the effect of predation helps to increase numbers.

Provided by
Habitat and predator management.

Partridges are particularly vulnerable to predation because they nest, forage and roost on the ground. Up to three-quarters of the potential reproduction for a year can be lost through egg predation[8,44]. We know that predation has become more of a problem for many farmland species in recent decades, particularly ground-nesting birds[28,29,140] and hares[40]. This may be because the number of generalist predators (those that eat whatever food is available to them) has increased overall during that period[28], or because the farmed landscape has become simpler, with fewer hedgerows and other features, or a combination of both. This simplification means that predator and prey species increasingly share the same areas and resources, and are therefore more likely to meet, with prey less able to hide[141].

GREY PARTRIDGES ARE VULNERABLE TO PREDATION

The grey partridge is a very short-lived species in comparison with other birds of similar size – its average life expectancy is thought to be only around 1.5 years[142]. This is because its life is typically curtailed through predation[6-8]. This means that most partridges will have only one opportunity to breed in their lifetime. During the breeding season the main partridge predator is the red fox[8] – but during the winter months, particularly during times of heavy snow, birds of prey are the main threat, especially sparrowhawk and goshawk[34,117,143,144]. As well as this, a range of other European predators also kill partridges. The famous German naturalist Alfred Brehm summed it up in the 1860s as follows: *'If one visualises the threats to which a grey partridge is exposed including all predators, it is hard to comprehend why partridges are actually still around'* [145].

The nesting female is particularly vulnerable to predation. In unmanaged areas, more than half of the females present may be lost during the breeding season[109,142,146]. Nesting success is therefore heavily influenced by predation[20,30]. Nest predation by generalist predators is generally density-dependent, which means that nest losses are relatively higher in areas with higher partridge densities compared to where there are fewer partridges, all else being equal[8]. Predation can suppress the growth of a low-density partridge population[141]. Local conditions, such as the density of other prey species, the distribution of nesting habitat and predator searching may counteract this. The most convincing study highlighting the influence of predation on partridge breeding numbers comes from an experiment carried out in England. There, where predator management was carried out during the breeding season, grey partridges produced more chicks and autumn numbers increased by 75% each year (this included all predators legally controllable under UK law, including foxes, corvids and mustelids). This increased spring breeding numbers, which were nearly three times higher on average after three years, compared to a nearby comparison area where breeding success was much lower[147].

Within PARTRIDGE we are very aware of the sensitive issues revolving around lethal predation management. The partnership includes those with different views, working within different legal frameworks in different countries with different socio-cultural backgrounds, reflecting the diversity found across European society. Therefore, the conservation methods used within PARTRIDGE are designed to be applied alongside either of the main predation management approaches. Each demonstration site chose the predation management approach that was most suitable for its particular situation and aims.

HABITAT MANAGEMENT TO LIMIT PREDATION

In grey partridge conservation projects where lethal predator management is not carried out, the effects of predation may be reduced through habitat improvements. This improvement is directed towards the amount, types and layout of nesting, brood-rearing and overwinter habitat to increase partridge survival. How these are implemented varies between sites. Up until now, there has been little scientific investigation into how exactly habitat management alone can best support sustainable partridge populations in the long-term.

One exception to this is a demonstration site in the UK, where low grey partridge numbers recovered and could be maintained with habitat management alone. This occurred in an area with low background predator densities[130]. The important things to consider are the size of the area being managed for conservation and how fragmented the areas of suitable nesting, brood-rearing and overwinter habitats are, as well as the background density of predators. The presence of partridges nearby is also likely to play an important role in buffering numbers[148].

PREDATION

Figure 5 Schematic representation of fluctuation in grey partridge numbers over the course of a year. Adapted from Pegel[142]. The exact timing and proportion of losses will vary depending on local conditions.

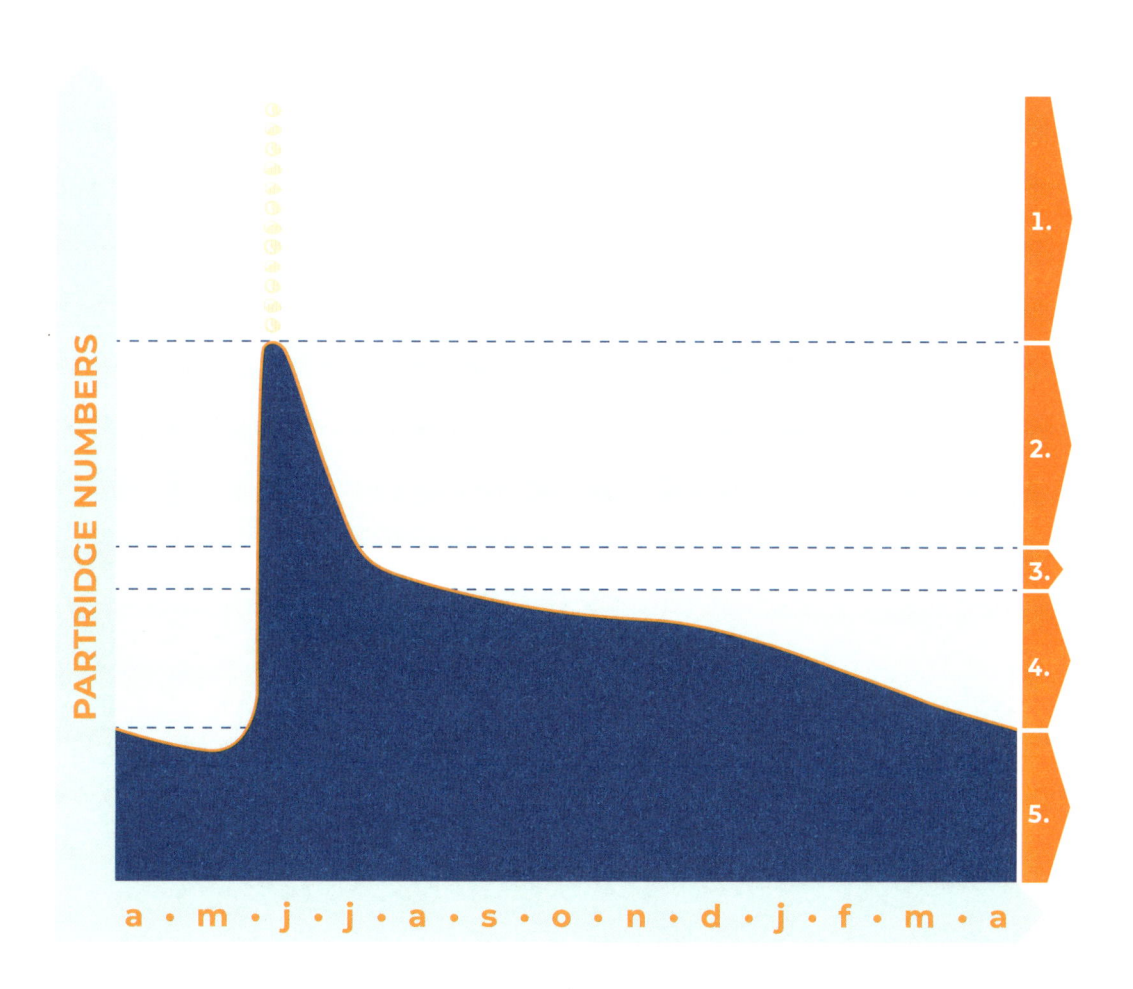

PARTRIDGE NUMBERS

a • m • j • j • a • s • o • n • d • j • f • m • a

1. 50% nest losses – eggs destroyed before hatching

2. 50% of hatched chicks lost

3. 30% of adults lost during the summer

4. 60% autumn and winter losses

5. The remaining partridges

Partridge female buried by fox Francis Buner

THE EVIDENCE for partridges

Adjusting habitat can help manage predation pressure. In a simple open landscape with fewer areas for wildlife to use, it is more likely that predator and prey will meet, than in a more complex landscape with many areas of suitable habitat[141]. Both the amount of good-quality habitat and its layout are important to reduce predation risk for partridges.

Computer modelling of UK partridge populations has predicted that numbers could be stabilised without predator control if 3% of the total arable area of the UK comprised insect-rich brood-rearing habitat and if there were 4.3 kilometres of nesting cover per 100 hectares[8,25]. The results of this modelling have, to date, not been experimentally demonstrated.

In Germany, the Göttinger Grey Partridge project, covering an area of 100,000 hectares, managed to hold the local grey partridge population stable at two pairs/100 hectares between 2007 and 2018, while in the rest of Lower Saxony numbers fell by half. This was achieved by adding 540 hectares of wildflower plots in blocks of up to one hectare to the suitable partridge habitat that already existed in the area. Lethal predator management was not part of the project, but fox control did occur at low levels as local hunters culled foxes during the winter as part of their existing routine[44]. Partridge numbers fluctuated greatly between years and between local areas, with some areas losing their partridges, then being re-colonised by partridges from nearby areas. A nine-fold increase from 0.6 to 5.6 pairs/100 hectares was recorded in one area of approximately 600 hectares, where the amount of newly-created high-quality habitat was 7%[44].

Nesting success can be heavily influenced by the structures provided for nesting habitat. In the Göttinger study, 62% of nests in linear structures such as hedgerows or field margins (10 metres wide or less) were predated. Wider structures provided more safety, with only 24% of the nests predated if they were located in structures more than 20 metres wide such as wildflower plots[44]. Narrow strips of good-quality partridge habitat can concentrate the birds into corridors, allowing ground predators to easily find them[51], with the nesting corridors acting as what is commonly called a 'predator trap'[49,149].

However, success based on habitat measures alone is not always possible, as a partridge recovery project in Switzerland showed. In the canton of Geneva, where lethal predator management is forbidden by law all year round, an attempt to minimise nest predation using electric

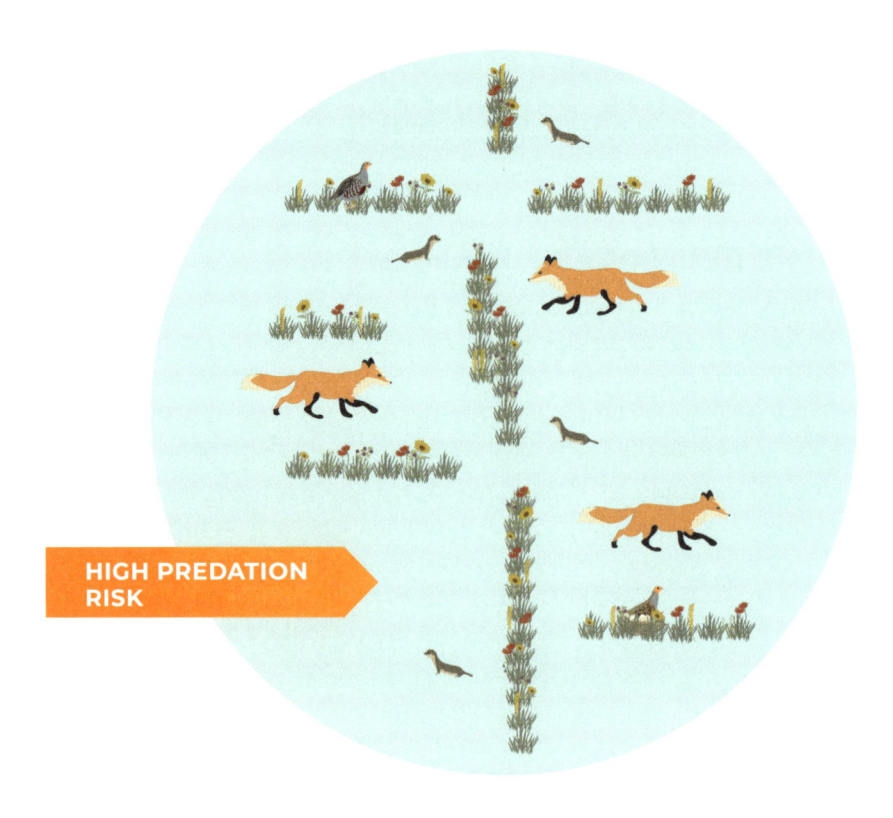

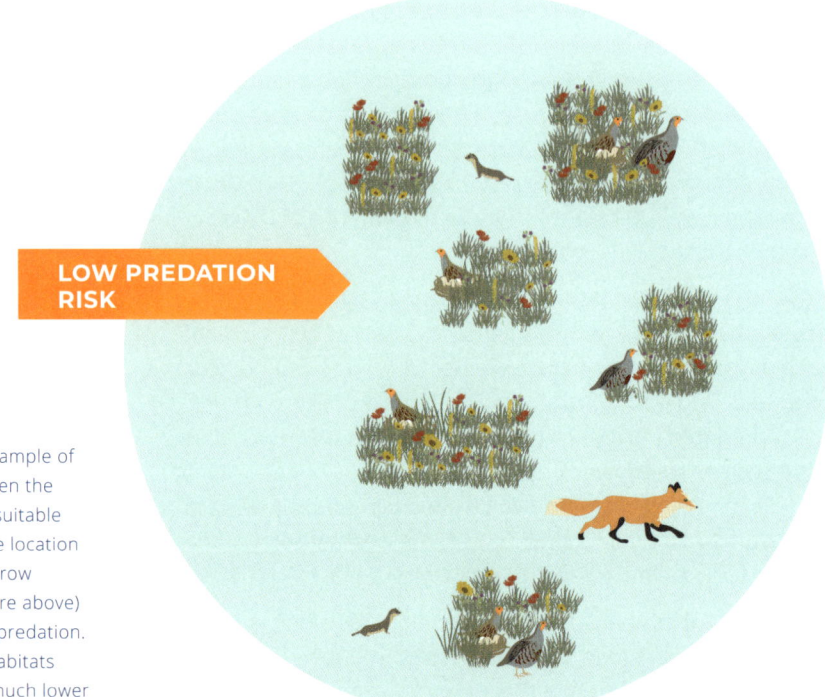

Figure 6 Schematic example of the relationship between the spatial distribution of suitable nesting habitat and the location of partridge nests. Narrow breeding habitats (figure above) result in a high risk of predation. Bigger block-shaped habitats (figure below) have a much lower risk of predation. Based on Gottschalk & Beeke[44].

fencing was unsuccessful despite increasing hatching success[150]. The grey partridge could not be saved from extinction, even with the provision of 5.3% high-quality insect-rich habitat, across an area of 10,000ha[132,148,168]. Notwithstanding habitat measures undertaken over a 15-year period, the project area was too isolated from the next known partridge population 70 kilometres away to be sustainable. Despite the release of reared grey partridges to supplement the wild population, from a starting point of two wild pairs on the study area in 2007, only three pairs were present in 2016[148,151] and the species was considered extinct in Switzerland in 2020[168].

For other species

The same Swiss study that failed to increase partridge numbers with habitat measures and nest fencing, did result in higher numbers of some other farmland birds. Six of twelve species studied increased over the study period: whitethroat, melodious warbler, stonechat, yellowhammer, red-backed shrike and cirl bunting[132].

One RSPB-run demonstration farm in the UK, where predator densities were relatively low, increased numbers of farmland birds through habitat management alone (including winter feeding)[130].

Excluding predators from nest sites of other species using physical barriers such as fencing has also been trialled and has been successful in some cases, for example protecting lapwing chicks in Switzerland[152,153], various meadow bird species in the Netherlands and waders across other parts of Europe[154].

There is also growing evidence that AE scheme measures, such as unimproved field margins[155–157] and wildflower blocks lead to reduced predation pressure, which benefits hares[64, 155-157].

PREDATOR MANAGEMENT TO MINIMISE PREDATION

As well as providing habitat to limit predation, where there are high levels of generalist predators, direct (i.e. lethal) predator management is widely used to protect vulnerable prey species. This is particularly the case in ground-nesting species such as seabirds, waders and gamebirds[28]. In the case of grey partridges, creating a shootable surplus is often the motivation behind the predator management[10,36].

Grey partridge recovery programmes that do not have shooting as motivation also use lethal predator management[41]. How this is done and which species are involved depends on the legal framework, which varies across European countries. Where legally permitted, predator management aims to reduce the density of generalist predators such as red fox and crow during the nesting season to ensure good partridge reproduction[80]. This type of management can be carried out successfully across relatively small areas, resulting in high grey partridge spring pair densities of up to 40-80 pairs per square kilometre[41,80,158].

Lowering predation pressure contributes to partridge and other farmland wildlife conservation. It can be achieved by making habitats more predation-proof and limiting predator access to nest sites, with the highest level of protection involving lethal predator control. The highest density of partridges is achieved where all of these management techniques are combined.

THE EVIDENCE for partridges

Where it is permitted, and carried out to the highest possible standard, combining lethal predator management with habitat measures leads to higher grey partridge numbers[80,158]. Early studies in the UK indicated that partridge numbers were higher where there was more gamekeeping[23,159].

These results were followed by a replicated controlled experimental field study where predator management was carried out only during the partridge breeding season. Grey partridge breeding success was higher and autumn numbers increased. This increased spring breeding numbers, which were on average nearly three times higher after three years, compared with a nearby reference area without predator management[147].

More recent analyses using computer models predict that combining habitat management with predator management as described above results in faster and higher grey partridge recovery than habitat measures alone[25,160]. This has been demonstrated several times in the UK, France and Ireland[41,48,80,121,158].

In cases where grey partridges are reintroduced after they had gone locally extinct, predator control is paramount for success. All known successful reintroductions of grey partridges in Europe that have been scientifically documented have used direct predator management, in addition to providing good-quality habitat across a suitable area.

Examples of successful reintroductions include one in Ireland[41] and one in the UK[161]. These reintroductions made the decision to undertake direct predator management in light of IUCN guidelines for introductions[162,163]. These state that the original reasons for extinction must be removed before reintroduction takes place. For the grey partridge, this includes high rates of predation as well as loss of habitat, and both must be suitably addressed for reintroduced birds to be able to persist[139].

For other species

Reducing predator numbers using legal lethal management to help grey partridges, eases the pressure on other species. Direct predator management for grey partridge conservation resulted in higher numbers of birds of conservation concern in two project areas in the UK[4,161] and on areas managed through the GWCT Partridge Count Scheme[38]. Direct predator management resulted in greater nesting success for five of six species nesting in hedgerows, including yellowhammer[164].

The usefulness of lethal predator management depends on the background density of predators present. In areas with high predator densities, predator management was required for songbird numbers to recover, whereas where there were fewer predators, habitat management was enough without predator management[130,164].

This has also been shown for lapwing, which bred better where generalist predators were removed in areas with a high background level of these predators[165]. In a recent review of whether predation can limit prey populations, removing predators allowed prey populations to rise in 80% of studies that looked at seabirds, 81% looking at gamebirds, 45% of those studying waders and 40% focusing on songbirds[28].

Reducing the density of common generalist predators such as foxes can also benefit brown hares. A combined analysis of three separate UK studies showed that in all three, brown hare densities increased rapidly and were always higher when predators were controlled than when they were not[40].

Brown hare along Swiss wildflower plot Markus Jenny

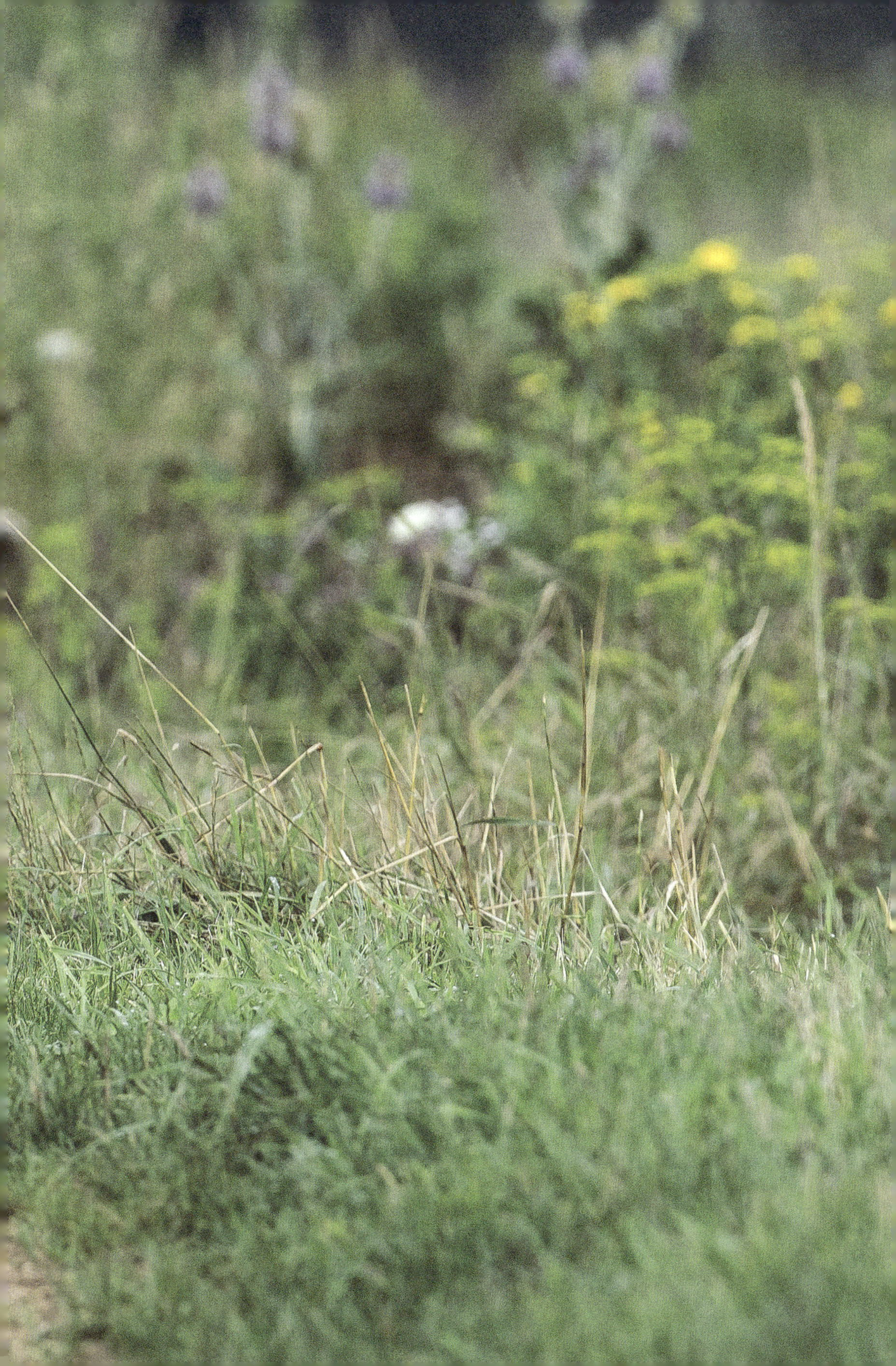

Ethics and science

Predator management is a highly debated topic across Europe. For many people, including much of the general public, the killing of one or more species for the benefit of others is ethically unacceptable. To others, such as some species conservation managers, lethally managing common predators to protect red-listed prey species is necessary to help these more vulnerable species to survive. For others still, such as hunters, lethal predator management allows high enough numbers of their quarry species for shooting, acting as a motivation for the habitat and predator management carried out to achieve this[166].

Ethics are beyond the scope of this booklet. Nevertheless, PARTRIDGE is very aware of the ethical issues that revolve around predator management. We therefore simply provide as concise and balanced a summary as possible of the current evidence concerning the effects of indirect and direct predator management practices across Europe.

PREDATION

Farm walk at Rotherfield demonstration site, England Ian Gould

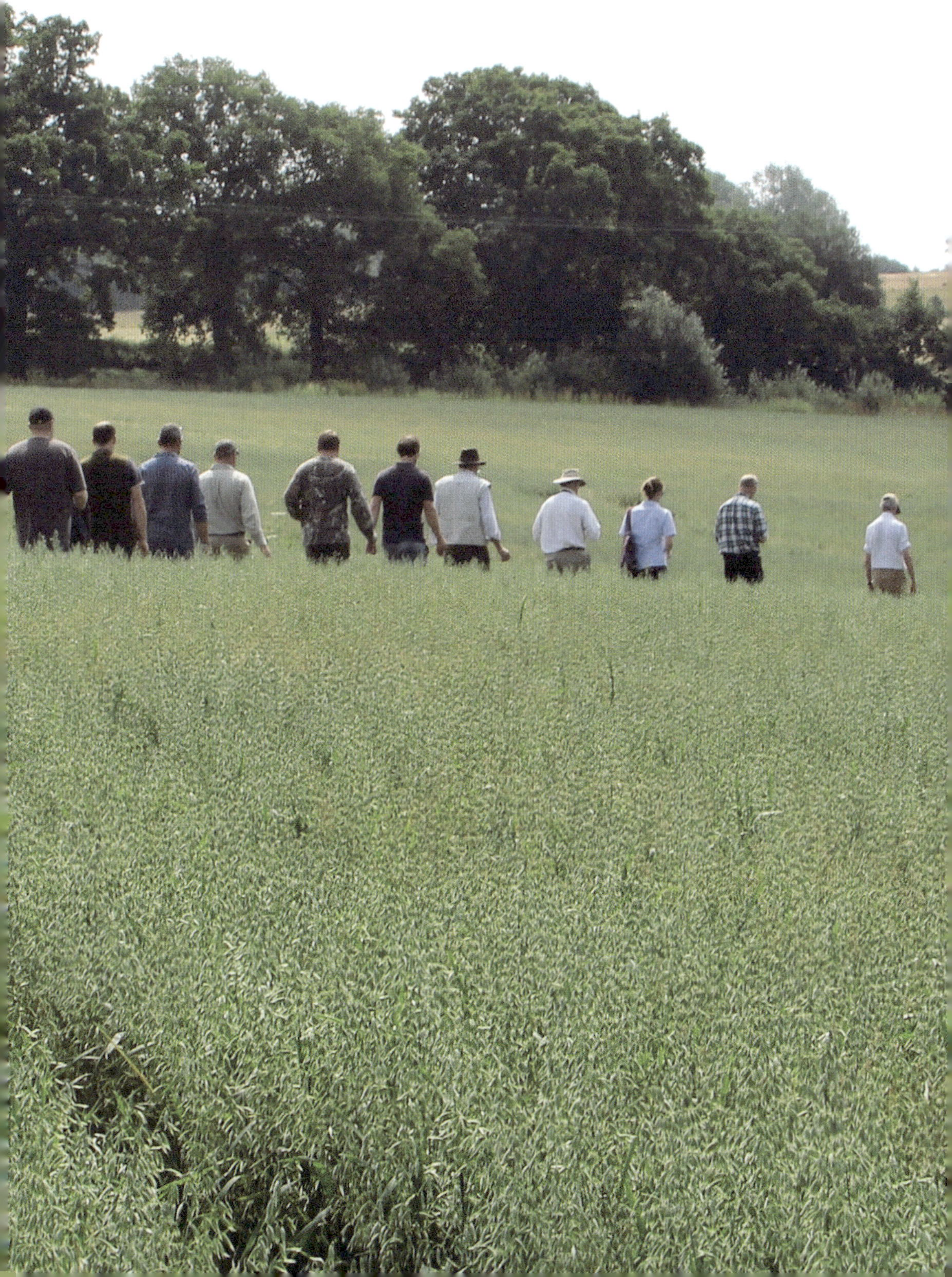

WORKING TOGETHER FOR A COMMON AIM

Successful conservation projects understand and respect the views of different groups with different priorities, values and ideas. Bringing together and uniting a wide range of stakeholders working together towards a common goal is what PARTRIDGE is all about. The main roles of the seven key stakeholder groups that need to work together are summarised below. Many people or groups fulfil several of these roles.

The following is based on characteristics of stakeholders involved in this project and others. It represents an ambitious, aspirational interpretation, but those who wish to restore numbers of grey partridges and other farmland wildlife should live up to these expectations to ensure success.

The role of the farmer

Farmers are the core component of PARTRIDGE. Those who manage the land have the ability to create and manage habitats for biodiversity. Many farmers have an intrinsic interest in wildlife and biodiversity. However, they must also run a profitable business and produce food. This is where AE scheme funding is extremely important as it compensates farmers for the income that is lost when they choose to use land for conservation rather than production.

Farmers and landowners working together, in farmer collectives in the Netherlands or Farmer Clusters in the UK, can produce conservation benefits over a large area.

Almost 100 farmers across our 10 demonstration sites manage all the PARTRIDGE habitat measures, while helping to showcase how farmland biodiversity can be restored alongside running a modern farm business.

The role of the hunter

Hunting and shooting organisations from several countries are key partners in PARTRIDGE. Hunters of small game (gamebirds and hares) have a strong motivation to conserve and support their quarry species, and other associated wildlife. Many hunters are keen conservationists and as such manage their quarry sustainably. Their understanding of and investment in the countryside can contribute to conservation projects.

In the UK, where the shooting rights lie with the landowner, this is straightforward. In other parts of Europe, such as France and Germany, the hunter may rent land from farmers to plant and manage wildlife habitats that benefit their quarry species, or may pay the farmer to provide these services.

Arrangements will vary, but hunters often make a contribution to management for quarry species. When this management is done in line with the appropriate guidelines and codes of practice, it benefits many other farmland species.

Sustainable shooting is an important aspect of how hunters manage quarry species. One example from the UK recommends that no grey partridges are shot unless there are more than 20 birds per 100 hectares in autumn, and that hunting stops for the year if that threshold is reached. In the UK, on areas with habitat management providing both nesting and brood-rearing cover, together with legal predator control, grey partridge numbers can sustain moderate shooting of 20% of autumn stocks[48,166]. In the modern farmed environment, there are unlikely to be that many wild partridges without either seven percent of high-quality habitat, direct predator management, or both.

PARTRIDGE partners with local stakeholders Francis Buner

The role of the general public

PARTRIDGE unites around 300 volunteers from the general public engaging in habitat management, monitoring activities (citizen science such as bird surveys), media campaigns and lobbying. They are typically members of conservation organisations, helping both financially and by adding a voice to the cause of conservation through support for conservation-friendly policy choices.

Pressure from our volunteers and the wider public is one of the most effective tools in achieving change and steering regional, national and international policy. Public appreciation for the work done by farmers and hunters can go a long way towards motivating land managers to undertake conservation work.

The role of the advisory body

Within PARTRIDGE, advice on AE schemes, wildlife and management is provided by a group of experts with different strengths. These advisors work together to offer a wide range of expertise and real-world experience, acting as a link between scientific and conservation organisations and land managers.

They understand both wildlife requirements and the details of running a farm business, effectively integrating new farming methods or conservation measures into a working farm. They help and support the application process for AE schemes, the financial support which makes implementing conservation measures possible for most farmers. It is important that advisors are respected and trusted by farmers, not only for their knowledge but also for their practical approach to implementation.

The role of the scientist

PARTRIDGE includes several scientific organisations that have researched and developed new techniques and conservation measures directed towards farmland conservation, as summarised in this publication. Producing the evidence that conservation measures are effective is crucial to the successful conservation of farmland biodiversity, but it must be combined with demonstrating how these measures can be incorporated into farming practice without hampering operational efficiency or business profitability.

Within PARTRIDGE, existing scientific evidence has guided the selection of measures implemented at the 10 demonstration sites. Monitoring biodiversity indicators provides the evidence that our measures work under a range of circumstances irrespective of borders and regional differences.

The role of the conservation organisation

Conservation bodies forge partnerships across different groups, are influential in directing policy and thus play a critical part in PARTRIDGE. They often manage nature reserves themselves so can demonstrate best practice and they can create connections that will lead to conservation change.

Conservation bodies effectively communicate to policy makers and the general public the benefit and importance of conservation. In PARTRIDGE they educate policy-makers on the researched conservation approaches used, so that these measures can be rapidly integrated into governmental policy and AE schemes.

The role of government

PARTRIDGE highlights the benefits of partridge conservation for policy makers in government and provides the evidence that they need to support farmland conservation. Policy makers are key to ensuring that the enthusiasm and resources provided by all the other PARTRIDGE partners results in widespread and long-lasting conservation improvements. Policy makers that understand the science and its application will enact appropriate legislation and provide financial support, allowing funding for techniques that give maximum benefit.

Co-operation

Co-operation - between groups and across countries - is a core value of PARTRIDGE, enabling us to achieve our joint vision of the best outcomes for wildlife and people. There are complex challenges when working across many countries. Not only language but traditions, culture and perspectives differ. However, the successful establishment of PARTRIDGE demonstrates the rewards that can come from international co-operation within conservation, based on science.

WHERE CAN I LEARN MORE?

All the latest news and results of the PARTRIDGE project can be found on the following webpages:

www.northsearegion.eu/partridge

www.gwct.org.uk

https://twitter.com/PARTRIDGE_NSR

In the UK, the PARTRIDGE wildflower mixes mentioned in this booklet are available from Oakbank Game & Conservation and Kings Crops.

www.oakbankgc.co.uk/wild-game

www.kingscrops.co.uk/products/conservation-crops/wild-bird-seed-mixes

Child with cornflower Lars Soerink

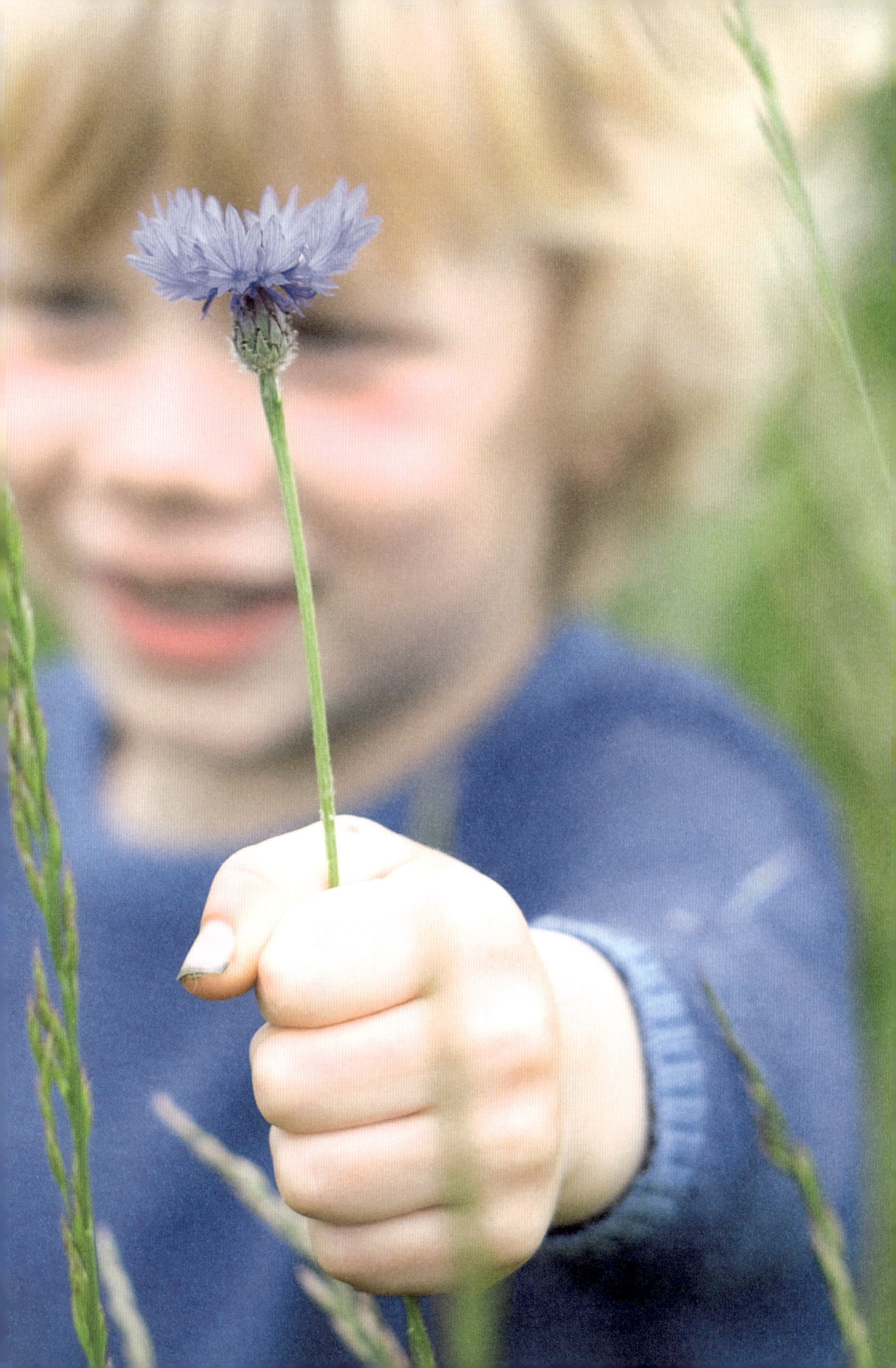

REFERENCES

REFERENCES

1 European Commission. (2011) *The EU Biodiversity Strategy to 2020*. Luxembourg.

2 European Commission. (2015) *Mid-term review of the EU biodiversity strategy to 2020*.

3 European Bird Census Council (EBCC). (2017) Trends of Common Birds in Europe, 2017 Update. Available at: http://ebcc.birdlife.cz/trends-of-common-birds-in-europe-2017-update/.

4 Potts, G.R. (2012) *Partridges. Countryside barometer. New Naturalist Library Book 121*. Collins. London.

5 European Environment Agency. (2004) *High Nature Value Farmland – Characteristics, Trends and Policy Challenges*. Copenhagen.

6 Birkan, M. & Jacob, M. (1988) *La Perdix Grise*. Hatier. Paris.

7 Dwenger, R. (1991) *Das Rebhuhn. Die Neue Brehm-Bücherei, Band 447*. Ziemsen Verlag. Wittenberg Lutherstadt.

8 Potts, G.R. (1986) *The Partridge. Pesticides, Predation and Conservation*. Collins. London.

9 Szederjei, A., Szederjei, M. & La'szio, S. (1959) *Hasen, Rebhühner, Fasane*. Deutscher Bauernverlag. Berlin.

10 Kuijper, D.P.J., Oosterveld, E. & Wymenga, E. (2009) Decline and potential recovery of the European grey partridge (*Perdix perdix*) population – a review. *European Journal of Wildlife Research*, **55:** 455–463.

11 Potts, G.R. & Aebischer, N.J. (1995) Population dynamics of the grey partridge *Perdix perdix* 1793–1993: monitoring, modelling and management. *Ibis*, **137:** S29-37.

12 Bijlsma, R.G., Hustings, F. & Camphuysen, C.J. (2001) *Algemene en schaarse broedvogels van Nederland. Avifauna van Nederland, 2*. GMB Uitgeverij/KNNV Uitgeverij. Haarlem/Utrecht.

13 Sovon. (2018) *Vogelatlas van Nederland. Broedvogels, wintervogels en 40 jaar verandering. (Dutch Bird Atlas)*. Kosmos Uitgevers. Utrecht/Antwerpen.

14 Sovon Partridge. Available at: https://www.sovon.nl/nl/soort/3670.

15 Sotherton, N.W. (1991) Conservation Headlands: a practical combination of intensive cereal farming and conservation. In: *Ecology of Temperate Cereal Fields*: 373–397. (eds. Firbank, L.G., Carter, N., Darbyshire, J.F. & Potts, G.R.) British Ecological Society Symposium, Blackwell Scientific Publications. Oxford.

16 Southwood, T.R.E. & Cross, D.J. (2002) Food requirements of grey partridge *Perdix perdix* chicks. *Wildlife Biology*, **8:** 175–183.

17 Ford, J., Chitty, H. & Middleton, A.D. (1938) The food of partridge chicks *(Perdix perdix)* in Great Britain. *The Journal of Animal Ecology*, **7:** 251–265.

18 Potts, G.R. & Aebischer, N.J. (1991) Modelling the population dynamics of the grey partridge: conservation and management. In: *Bird Population Studies: Their Relevance to Conservation and Management*: 373–390. (eds. Perrins, C.M., Lebreton, J.D. & Hirons, G.J.M.) Oxford University Press. Oxford.

19 Carson, R. (1962) *Silent Spring*. Houghton Mifflin Company. Oxford.

20 Bro, E. & Millot, F. (2013) Bilan de l'étude PeGASE sur la perdrix grise. *Faune Sauvage*, **298:** 17–48.

21 Ewald, J.A., Wheatley, C.J., Aebischer, N.J., Moreby, S.J., Duffield, S.J., Crick, H.Q.P. & Morecroft, M.B. (2015) Influences of extreme weather, climate and pesticide use on invertebrates in cereal fields over 42 years. *Global Change Biology*, **21:** 3931–3950.

22 Aebischer, N.J. & Potts, G.R. (1998) Spatial changes in grey partridge (*Perdix perdix*) distribution in relation to 25 years of changing agriculture in Sussex, U.K. *Gibier Faune Sauvage*, **15:** 293–308.

23 Potts, G.R. (1980) The effects of modern agriculture, nest predation and game management on the population ecology of partridges. *Advances in Ecological Research*, **11:** 1–79.

24 Rands, M. (1986) Effect of hedgerow characteristics on partridge breeding densities. *Journal of Applied Ecology,* **23:** 479-487.

25 Aebischer, N.J. & Ewald, J.A. (2004) Managing the UK grey partridge *Perdix perdix* recovery: population change, reproduction, habitat and shooting. *Ibis,* **146:** 181-191.

26 Teunissen, W., Roodbergen, M., van den Bremer, L., Sierdsema, H. & de Jong, A. (2014) *Jaar van de Patrijs 2013. Sovon-rapport 2014/26.* Nijmegen. (Report in Dutch).

27 Tapper, S.C. (1999) *A Question of Balance - Game Animals and Their Role in the British Countryside.* The Game Conservancy Trust. Fordingbridge.

28 Roos, S., Smart, J., Gibbons, D.W. & Wilson, J.D. (2018) A review of predation as a limiting factor for bird populations in mesopredator-rich landscapes: A case study of the UK. *Biological Reviews:* doi:10.1111/brv.12426

29 Bro, E., Sarrazin, F., Clobert, J. & Reitz, F. (2000) Demography and the decline of the grey partridge *Perdix perdix* in France. *Journal of Applied Ecology,* **37:** 432-448.

30 Panek, M. (2005) Demography of grey partridges *Perdix perdix* in Poland in the years 1991-2004: Reasons of population decline. *European Journal of Wildlife Research,* **51:** 14-18.

31 Faragó, S., Dittrich, G., Horváth-Hangya, K. & Winkler, D. (2012) Twenty years of the grey partridge population in the LAJTA Project (Western Hungary). *Animal Biodiversity and Conservation,* **35:** 311-319.

32 Carroll, J.P. (1992) A model of Gray Partridge *(Perdix perdix)* population dynamics in North Dakota. In: Perdix VI: First International Symposium on Partridges, Quails and Francolins; *Gibier Faune Sauvage:* **9:** 337-349. (eds. Birkan, M.G., Potts, G.R., Aebischer, N.J. & Dowell, S.D.) Office National de la Chasse. Paris.

33 Meriggi, A., Saino, N., Montagna, D. & Zacchetti, D. (1992) Influence of habitat on density and breeding success of grey and red-legged partridges. *Italian Journal of Zoology,* **59:** 289-295.

34 Buner, F.D. & Aebisher, N.J. (2011) Grey partridge winter losses. *GWCT Annual Review,* **43:** 36-37.

35 Roodbergen, M. (2013) *Het Jaar van de Patrijs: kennisupdate. Sovon-rapport 2013/12.* Nijmegen. (Report in Dutch).

36 Aebischer, N.J. & Ewald, J.A. (2012) The grey partridge in the UK: population status, research, policy and prospects. *Animal Biodiversity and Conservation,* **35:** 353-362.

37 Sotherton, N.W., Aebischer, N.J. & Ewald, J.A. (2014) Research into action: grey partridge conservation as a case study. *Journal of Applied Ecology,* **51:** 1-5.

38 Connor, H.E. & Draycott, R.A.H. (2010) Management strategies to conserve the grey partridge: the effect on other farmland birds. *Aspects of Applied Biology,* **100:** 359-363.

39 Ewald, J.A., Aebischer, N.J., Moreby, S.J. & Potts, G.R. (2015) Changes in the cereal ecosystem on the South Downs of southern England, over the past 45 years. *Aspects of Applied Biology,* **128:** 11-19.

40 Reynolds, J.C., Stoate, C., Brockless, M.H., Aebischer, N.J. & Tapper, S.C. (2010) The consequences of predator control for brown hares *(Lepus europaeus)* on UK farmland. *European Journal of Wildlife Research,* **56:** 541-549.

41 Buckley, K., Kelly, P., Kavanagh, B., O'Gorman, E.C., Carnus, T. & McMahon, B.J. (2012) Every partridge counts, successful techniques used in the captive conservation breeding programme for wild grey partridge in Ireland. *Animal Biodiversity and Conservation,* **35:** 387-393.

42 Kuijper, D.J.P. (2007) *De Patrijs in Nederland. Oorzaken van achteruitgang en mogelijkheden voor herstel. A&W-rapport 931.* Veenwoude.

43 Bro, E., Reitz, F. & Clobert, J. (2000) Nest-site selection of grey partridge *(Perdix perdix)* on agricultural lands in North-Central France. *Game and Wildlife Science*, **17**: 1–16.

44 Gottschalk, E. & Beeke, W. (2014) How can the drastic decline in the grey partridge *(Perdix perdix)* be stopped? Lessons from ten years of the Grey Partridge Conservation Project in the district of Göttingen. *Berichte zum Vogelschutz*, **51**: 95–116.

45 Buner, F.D., Jenny, M., Zbinden, N. & Naef-Daenzer, B. (2005) Ecologically enhanced areas - A key habitat structure for re-introduced grey partridges *Perdix perdix*. *Biological Conservation*, **124**: 373–381.

46 Aebischer, N.J., Blake, K.A. & Boatman, N.D. (1994) Field margins as habitats for game. In: *Field Margins: Integrating Agriculture and Conservation*: 95–104. (ed. Boatman, N.D.) BCPC Monograph No. 58, British Crop Protection Council. Farnham.

47 Panek, M. (1997) Density-dependent brood production in the Grey Partridge *Perdix perdix* in relation to habitat quality. *Bird Study*, **44**: 235–238.

48 Aebischer, N.J. & Ewald, J.A. (2010) Grey partridge *Perdix perdix* in the UK: recovery status, set-aside and shooting. *Ibis*, **152**: 530–542.

49 Rantanen, E.M.I., Buner, F., Riordan, P., Sotherton, N.W. & Macdonald, D.W. (2010) Habitat preferences and survival in wildlife reintroductions: an ecological trap in reintroduced grey partridges. *Journal of Applied Ecology*, **47**: 1357–1364.

50 Buner, F.D., Aebisher, N.J. & Brockless, M.H. (2010) The Rotherfield demonstration project. *GWCT Annual Review*, **42**: 22–25.

51 Šálek, M., Kreisinger, J., Sedláček, F. & Albrecht, T. (2009) Corridor vs. hayfield matrix use by mammalian predators in an agricultural landscape. *Agriculture, Ecosystems and Environment*, **134**: 8–13.

52 Maudsley, M.J. (2000) A review of the ecology and conservation of hedgerow invertebrates in Britain. *Journal of Environmental Management*, **60**: 65–76.

53 Dover, J.W. (2019) *The Ecology of Hedgerows and Field Margins*. Routledge. Abingdon.

54 Kennedy, C.E.J. & Southwood, T.R.E. (1984) The number of species of insects associated with British trees: a re-analysis. *The Journal of Animal Ecology*, **53**: 455–478.

55 Dover, J.W. & Sparks, T.H. (2000) A review of the ecology of butterflies in British hedgerows. *Journal of Environmental Management*, **60**: 51–63.

56 Dunn, J.C., Gruar, D., Stoate, C., Szczur, J. & Peach, W.J. (2016) Can hedgerow management mitigate the impacts of predation on songbird nest survival? *Journal of Environmental Management*, **184**: 535–544.

57 Thomas, S.R., Goulson, D. & Holland, J.M. (2000) The contribution of beetle banks to farmland biodiversity. *Aspects of Applied Biology*, **58**: 31–38.

58 Collins, K.L., Boatman, N.D., Wilcox, A., Holland, J.M. & Chaney, K. (2002) Influence of beetle banks on cereal aphid predation in winter wheat. *Agriculture, Ecosystems and Environment*, **93**: 337–350.

59 Tillman, P.G., Smith, H.A. & Holland, J.M. (2012) Cover crops and related methods for enhancing agricultural biodiversity and conservation biocontrol: successful case studies. In: *Biodiversity and Insect Pests: Key Issues for Sustainable Management*: 309–327. (eds. Gurr, G., Wratten, S., Snyder, W. & Read, D.) Wiley-Blackwell. Oxford. doi:10.1002/9781118231838.ch19

60 Thomas, M.B., Wratten, S.D. & Sotherton, N.W. (1991) Creation of 'island' habitats in farmland to manipulate populations of beneficial arthropods: predator densities and emigration. *Journal of Applied Ecology*, **28**: 906–917.

61 Bence, S.L., Stander, K. & Griffiths, M. (2003) Habitat characteristics of harvest mouse nests on arable farmland. *Agriculture, Ecosystems & Environment*, **99**: 179–186.

62 Vickery, J., Carter, N. & Fuller, R.J. (2002) The potential value of managed cereal field margins as foraging habitats for farmland birds in the UK. *Agriculture, Ecosystems and Environment,* **89:** 41–52.

63 Aschwanden, J., Holzgang, O. & Jenni, L. (2007) Importance of ecological compensation areas for small mammals in intensively farmed areas. *Wildlife Biology,* **13:** 150–158.

64 Hummel, S., Meyer, L., Hackländer, K. & Weber, D. (2017) Activity of potential predators of European hare *(Lepus europaeus)* leverets and ground-nesting birds in wildflower strips. *European Journal of Wildlife Research,* **63:** 102–115.

65 Hallmann, C.A., Sorg, M., Jongejans, E., Siepel, H., Hofland, N., Schwan, H., Stenmans, W., Müller, A., Sumser, H., Hörren, T., Goulson, D. & De Kroon, H. (2017) More than 75 percent decline over 27 years in total flying insect biomass in protected areas. PLoS ONE, **12:** e0185809.

66 Potts, G.R., Ewald, J.A. & Aebischer, N.J. (2010) Long term changes in the flora of the cereal ecosystem on the Sussex Downs, England, focusing on the years 1968–2005. *Journal of Applied Ecology,* **47:** 215–226.

67 Ewald, J.A., Wheatley, C.J., Aebischer, N.J., Duffield, S. & Heaver, D. (2016) *Investigation of the impact of changes in pesticide use on invertebrate populations. Natural England Commissioned Report, NECR182.* York.

68 Rands, M.R.W. (1986) The survival of gamebird *(Galliformes)* chicks in relation to pesticide use on cereals. *Ibis,* **128:** 57–64.

69 Ullrich, K.S. & Edwards, P.J. (1999) The colonization of wildflower strips by insects *(Heteroptera).* In: *Heterogeneity in landscape ecology: pattern and scale: Proc 8th annual IALE (UK) conference:* 131–138. (eds. Maudsley, M. & Marshall, J.) University of Bristol.

70 Ullrich, K.S. (2001) The influence of wildflower strips on plant and insect *(Heteroptera)* diversity in an arable landscape. ETH Zurich, PhD thesis.

71 Parish, D. & Sotherton, N.W. (2004) Game crops and threatened farmland songbirds in Scotland : a step towards halting population declines? *Bird Study,* **51:** 107–112.

72 Stoate, C., Henderson, I. & Parish, D.M. (2004) Development of an agri-environment scheme option: seed-bearing crops for farmland birds. *Ibis,* **146:** 203–209.

73 Henderson, I.G., Vickery, J.A. & Carter, N. (2004) The use of winter bird crops by farmland birds in lowland England. *Biological Conservation,* **118:** 21–32.

74 Parish, D. & Sotherton, N.W. (2004) Game crops as summer habitat for farmland songbirds in Scotland. *Agriculture, Ecosystems and Environment:* **104:** 429–438.

75 Lemanski, K. (2008) Vergleich der Arthropodenzusammensetzung in der Krautschicht auf Acker, Brache, einjährigen und mehrjährigen Blühstreifen in Hinblick auf die Nutzung als Nahrungsgrundlage von Rebhuhnküken *(Perdix perdix L.)* im Landkreis Göttingen. Universität Göettingen.

76 Maas, D.W. & van der Arend, I.E. (2018) *Insecten als voedselbron. Insecten-onderzoek binnen het Interreg-project PARTRIDGE. NatureToday bericht 3 juli 2018, Insectenexplosie bij PARTRIDGE, met bijlage.*

77 Ewald, J.A., Aebischer, N.J., Richardson, S.M., Grice, P. V. & Cooke, A.I. (2010) The effect of agri-environment schemes on grey partridges at the farm level in England. *Agriculture, Ecosystems and Environment,* **138:** 55–63.

78 Rands, M. (1985) Pesticide use on cereals and the survival of grey partridge chicks: a field experiment. *Journal of Applied Ecology,* **22:** 49–54.

79 Sotherton, N.W., Robertson, P.A. & Dowell, S.D. (1993) Manipulating pesticide use to increase the production of wild gamebirds in Britain. In: *Quail III: National Quail Symposium* 92–101.

80 Ewald, J.A., Potts, G.R. & Aebischer, N.J. (2012) Restoration of a wild grey partridge shoot: a major development in the Sussex study, UK. *Animal Biodiversity and Conservation,* **35:** 363–369.

81 Meek, B., Loxton, D., Sparks, T., Pywell, R., Pickett, H. & Nowakowski, M. (2002) The effect of arable field margin composition on invertebrate biodiversity. *Biological Conservation,* **106:** 259–271.

82 Frank, T. (1998) Attractiveness of sown weed strips on hoverflies *(Syrphidae, Diptera),* butterflies *(Rhopalocera, Lepidoptera),* wild bees *(Apoidea, Hymenoptera)* and thread-waisted wasps *(Sphecidae, Hymenoptera). Mitteilungen der Schweizerischen Entomologischen Gesellschaft,* **71:** 11–20.

83 van Alebeek, F. (2015) *Duurzaamheidseffecten van akkerranden. Wetenschappelijke en praktische onderbouwing van duurzaamheidsaspecten van akkerranden.* Wageningen UR - PPO-AGV, 21 pp.

84 Dicks, L.V., Ashpole, J.E., Dänhardt, J., James, K., Jönsson, A., Randall, N., Showler, D.A., Smith, R.K., Turpie, S., Williams, D.R. & Sutherland, W.J. (2018) Farmland Conservation. In: *What Works in Conservation:* 245–284. (eds. Sutherland, W.J., Dicks, L.V., Ockendon, N., Petrovan, S.O. & Smith, R.K.) Open Book Publishers. Cambridge, UK.

85 Briner, T., Nentwig, W. & Airoldi, J.P. (2005) Habitat quality of wildflower strips for common voles *(Microtus arvalis)* and its relevance for agriculture. *Agriculture, Ecosystems and Environment,* **105:** 173–179.

86 Aschwanden, J. & Buner, F.D. (2006) Ökologische Ausgleichsflächen, Kleinsäuger, Turmfalken *Falco tinnunculus* und Waldohreulen *Asio otus. Der Ornithologische Beobachter,* **103:** 57–58.

87 Redhead, J.W., Hinsley, S.A., Beckmann, B.C., Broughton, R.K. & Pywell, R.F. (2018) Effects of agri-environmental habitat provision on winter and breeding season abundance of farmland birds. *Agriculture, Ecosystems and Environment,* **251:** 114–123.

88 Weibel, U. (1999) Effects of wildflower strips in an intensively used arable area on skylarks *(Alauda arvensis).* Swiss Federal Institute of Technology, Zurich. PhD thesis.

89 Brickle, N.W., Harper, D.G.C., Aebischer, N.J. & Cockayne, S.H. (2000) Effects of agricultural intensification on the breeding success of corn buntings *Miliaria calandra. Journal of Applied Ecology,* **37:** 742–755.

90 Frank, T. & Nentwig, W. (1995) Ground dwelling spiders *(Araneae)* in sown weed strips and adjacent fields. *Acta Oecologica,* **16:** 179–193.

91 Haaland, C., Naisbit, R.E. & Bersier, L.F. (2011) Sown wildflower strips for insect conservation: a review. *Insect Conservation and Diversity,* **4:** 60–80.

92 Frank, T. (1997) Species diversity of ground beetles *(Carabidae)* in sown weed strips and adjacent fields. *Biological Agriculture and Horticulture,* **15:** 297–307.

93 Frank, T. (1999) Density of adult hoverflies *(Dipt., Syrphidae)* in sown weed strips and adjacent fields. *Journal of Applied Entomology,* **123:** 351–355.

94 Scheid, B.E. (2010) The role of sown wildflower strips for biological control in agroeco-systems. University of Göttingen. PhD thesis.

95 Nentwig, W., Frank, T. & Lethmayer, C. (1998) Sown weed strips: artificial ecological compensation areas as an important tool in conservation biological control. In: *Conservation Biological Control:* 133–153. (ed. Barbosa, P.) Academic Press. San Diego.

96 Dover, J.W., Sotherton, N.W. & Gobbett, K. (1990) Reduced pesticide inputs on cereal field margins: the effects on butterfly abundance. *Ecological Entomology,* **15:** 17–24.

97 Rands, M.R.W. & Sotherton, N.W. (1986) Pesticide use on cereal crops and changes in the abundance of butterflies on arable farmland in England. *Biological Conservation,* **36:** 71–82.

98 Dover, J.W. (1997) Conservation headlands: effects on butterfly distribution and behaviour. *Agriculture, Ecosystems and Environment,* **63:** 31-49.

99 Cowgill, S.E., Wratten, S.D. & Sotherton, N.W. (1993) The effect of weeds on the numbers of hoverfly (Diptera: Syrphidae) adults and the distribution and composition of their eggs in winter wheat. *Annals of Applied Biology,* **123:** 499-515.

100 Tew, T.E., Macdonald, D.W. & Rands, M.R.W. (1992) Herbicide application affects microhabitat use by arable wood mice (*Apodemus sylvaticus*). *Journal of Applied Ecology,* **29:** 532-539.

101 Still, K. & Byfield, A. (2010) Is Environmental Stewardship working for rare and threatened plants? *Aspects of Applied Biology,* **100:** 279-286.

102 Meyer, S., Wesche, K., Leuschner, C., van Elsen, T. & Metzner, J. (2010) A new conservation strategy for arable plant vegetation in Germany - the project '100 fields for biodiversity'. *Plant Breeding and Seed Science,* **61:** 25-34.

103 van Alebeek, F., Visser, A. & van den Broek, R. (2007) Akkerranden als (winter) schuilplaats voor natuurlijke vijanden. *Entomologische Berichten,* **67:** 223-225.

104 Vickery, J.A., Feber, R.E. & Fuller, R.J. (2009) Arable field margins managed for biodiversity conservation: a review of food resource provision for farmland birds. *Agriculture, Ecosystems and Environment,* **133:** 1-13.

105 Longley, M. & Sotherton, N.W. (1997) Measurements of pesticide spray drift deposition into field boundaries and hedgerows: 2. Autumn applications. *Environmental Toxicology and Chemistry,* **16:** 173-178.

106 Longley, M., Čilgi, T., Jepson, P.C. & Sotherton, N.W. (1997) Measurements of pesticide spray drift deposition into field boundaries and hedgerows: 1. Summer applications. *Environmental Toxicology and Chemistry,* **16:** 165-172.

107 Carluer, N., Tournebize, J., Gouy, V., Margoum, C., Vincent, B. & Gril, J.J. (2011) Role of buffer zones in controlling pesticides fluxes to surface waters. *Procedia Environmental Sciences,* **9:** 21-26.

108 Watson, M., Aebischer, N.J. & Cresswell, W. (2007) Vigilance and fitness in grey partridges *Perdix perdix*: the effects of group size and foraging-vigilance trade-offs on predation mortality. *Journal of Animal Ecology,* **76:** 211-221.

109 Reitz, F., Bro, E., Mayot, P. & Migot, P. (1999) Influence de l'habitat et de la prédation sur la démographie des perdrix grises. *Bulletin Mensuel de l'Office National de la Chasse,* **240:** 10-21.

110 Holland, J.M., Smith, B.M., Southway, S.E., Birkett, T.C. & Aebischer, N.J. (2008) The effect of crop, cultivation and seed addition for birds on surface weed seed densities in arable crops during winter. *Weed Research,* **48:** 503-511.

111 Siriwardena, G.M., Calbrade, N.A. & Vickery, J.A. (2008) Farmland birds and late winter food: does seed supply fail to meet demand? *Ibis,* **150:** 585-595.

112 Orlowski, G., Czarnecka, J. & Panek, M. (2011) Autumn-winter diet of Grey Partridges *Perdix perdix* in winter crops, stubble fields and fallows. *Bird Study,* **58:** 473-86.

113 Draycott, R.A.H., Hoodless, A.N., Ludiman, M.N. & Robertson, P.A. (1998) Effects of spring feeding on body condition of captive-reared ring-necked pheasants in Great Britain. *The Journal of Wildlife Management,* **62:** 557-563.

114 Wilson, J.D., Taylor, R. & Muirhead, L.B. (1996) Field use by farmland birds in winter: an analysis of field type preferences using resampling methods. *Bird Study,* **43:** 320-332.

115 Robinson, R.A. & Sutherland, W.J. (2002) Post-war changes in arable farming and biodiversity in Great Britain. *Journal of Applied Ecology,* **39:** 157-176.

116 Evans, A. (1997) The importance of mixed farming for seed-eating birds in the UK. In: *Farming and birds in Europe*: 150–177. (eds. Pain, D.J. & Pienkowski, M.W.) Academic Press. London.

117 Watson, M., Aebischer, N.J., Potts, G.R. & Ewald, J.A. (2007) The relative effects of raptor predation and shooting on overwinter mortality of grey partridges in the United Kingdom. *Journal of Applied Ecology*, **44**: 972–982.

118 Rymešová, D., Šmilauer, P. & Šálek, M. (2012) Sex- and age-biased mortality in wild Grey Partridge *Perdix perdix* populations. *Ibis*, **154**: 815–824.

119 Draycott, R.A.H., Woodburn, M.I.A., Carroll, J.P. & Sage, R.B. (2005) Effects of spring supplementary feeding on population density and breeding success of released pheasants *Phasianus colchicus* in Britain. *Wildlife Biology*, **11**: 177–182.

120 Hoodless, A.N., Draycott, R.A.H., Ludiman, M.N. & Robertson, P.A. (1999) Effects of supplementary feeding on territoriality, breeding success and survival of pheasants. *Journal of Applied Ecology*, **36**: 147–156.

121 Bourdouxhe, L. (2002) Cent quintaux, cent perdreaux. *Chasse et Nature*, **94**: 21–24.

122 Eraud, C., Cadet, E., Powolny, T., Gaba, S., Bretagnolle, F. & Bretagnolle, V. (2015) Weed seeds, not grain, contribute to the diet of wintering skylarks in arable farmlands of Western France. *European Journal of Wildlife Research*, **61**: 151–161.

123 Moorcroft, D., Whittingham, M.J., Bradbury, R.B. & Wilson, J.D. (2002) The selection of stubble fields by wintering granivorous birds reflects vegetation cover and food abundance. *Journal of Applied Ecology*, **39**: 535–547.

124 Hammers, M., Müskens, G.J.D.M., van Kats, R.J.M., Teunissen, W.A. & Kleijn, D. (2015) Ecological contrasts drive responses of wintering farmland birds to conservation management. *Ecography*, **38**: 813–821.

125 Pfiffner, L. & Luka, H. (2000) Overwintering of arthropods in soils of arable fields and adjacent semi-natural habitats. *Agriculture, Ecosystems & Environment*, **78**: 215–222.

126 Pywell, R.F., Shaw, L., Meek, W., Turk, A., Shore, R.F. & Nowakowski, M. (2007) Do wild bird seed mixtures benefit other taxa? *Aspects of Applied Biology*, **81**: 69–76.

127 Siriwardena, G.M., Stevens, D.K., Anderson, G.Q.A., Vickery, J.A., Calbrade, N.A. & Dodd, S. (2007) The effect of supplementary winter seed food on breeding populations of farmland birds: evidence from two large-scale experiments. *Journal of Applied Ecology*, **44**: 920–932.

128 Sanchez-Garcia, C., Buner, F.D. & Aebischer, N.J. (2015) Supplementary winter food for gamebirds through feeders: which species actually benefit? *Journal of Wildlife Management*, **79**: 832–845.

129 Stoate, C. & Szczur, J. (2009) Predation, winter feeding and songbirds. *GWCT Annual Review*, **41**: 56–57.

130 Aebischer, N.J., Bailey, C.M., Gibbons, D.W., Morris, A.J., Peach, W.J. & Stoate, C. (2016) Twenty years of local farmland bird conservation: the effects of management on avian abundance at two UK demonstration sites. *Bird Study*, **63**: 10–30.

131 Stoate, C. (2012) Filling the hungry gap - late-winter supplementary feeding of farmland birds. *Conservation Land Management*, 10:4–7.

132 Meichtry-Stier, K.S., Duplain, J., Lanz, M., Lugrin, B. & Birrer, S. (2018) The importance of size, location, and vegetation composition of perennial fallows for farmland birds. *Ecology and Evolution*, **8**: 9270–9281.

133 Broggi, M.F. & Willi, G. (1997) Abklärung Mindestbedarf von naturnahen Ausgleichsflächen in landwirtschaftlichen Gunstlagen des liechtensteinischen Alpenrheintals. *Berichte der Botanisch-Zoologischen Gesellschaft Liechtenstein-Sargans-Werdenberg*, **24**: 237–302.

134 Broggi, M.F. & Schlegel, H. (1990) *Minimum requis de surfaces proches de l'état naturel dans le paysage rural: illustré par l'exemple du plateau Suisse.* Zürich.

135 European Commission. (2013) Regulation (EU) No. 1307/2013 of the European Parliament and of the Council of 17 December 2013 establishing rules for direct payments to farmers under support schemes within the framework of the common agricultural policy and repealing Council Regulation. *Official Journal of the European Union*, **L 347:** 608–670.

136 Henderson, I.G., Holland, J.M., Storkey, J., Lutman, P., Orson, J. & Simper, J. (2012) Effects of the proportion and spatial arrangement of un-cropped land on breeding bird abundance in arable rotations. *Journal of Applied Ecology*, **49:** 883–891.

137 Cormont, A., Siepel, H., Clement, J., Melman, T.C.P., WallisDeVries, M.F., van Turnhout, C.A.M., Sparrius, L.B., Reemer, M., Biesmeijer, J.C., Berendse, F. & de Snoo, G.R. (2016) Landscape complexity and farmland biodiversity: evaluating the CAP target on natural elements. *Journal for Nature Conservation*, **30:** 19–26.

138 Meichtry-Stier, K.S., Jenny, M., Zellweger-Fischer, J. & Birrer, S. (2014) Impact of landscape improvement by agri-environment scheme options on densities of characteristic farmland bird species and brown hare *(Lepus europaeus)*. *Agriculture, Ecosystems and Environment*, **189:** 101–109.

139 Buner, F.D. & Aebischer, N.J. (2008) *Guidelines for re-establishing grey partridges through releasing.* Game & Wildlife Conservation Trust. Fordingbridge.

140 Roodbergen, M., van der Werf, B. & Hötker, H. (2012) Revealing the contributions of reproduction and survival to the Europe-wide decline in meadow birds: review and meta-analysis. *Journal of Ornithology:* **153:** 53–74.

141 Panek, M. (2013) Landscape structure, predation of red foxes on grey partridges, and their spatial relations. *Central European Journal of Biology*, **8:** 1119–1126.

142 Pegel, M. (1987) Das Rebhuhn *(Perdix perdix L)* im Beziehungsgefüge seiner Um- and Mitweltfaktoren. *Arbetskreis Wildbiologie und Jagdwissenschaft an der Justus-Liebig-Universitat Giessen*, **18:** 121.

143 Dudzinski, W. (1990) The impact of predators on a partridge population in winter. In: *Transactions of the 19th IUGB Congress, Trondheim* Vol 1: 209–212. (ed. Myrberget, S.) Norwegian Institute for Nature Research. Trondheim.

144 Bro, E., Reitz, F., Clobert, J., Migot, P. & Massot, M. (2001) Diagnosing the environmental causes of the decline in grey partridge *Perdix perdix* survival in France. *Ibis*, **143:** 120–132.

145 Neumann, C.W. (1924) *Brehms Tierleben in Auswahl. Band 5, Vögel 2*. Verlag von Philipp Reclam jun. Leipzig.

146 Panek, M. (2002) Space use, nesting sites and breeding success of grey partridge *(Perdix perdix)* in two agricultural management systems in western Poland. *Game and Wildlife Science*, **19:** 313–326.

147 Tapper, S.C., Potts, G.R. & Brockless, M.H. (1996) The effect of an experimental reduction in predation pressure on the breeding success and population density of grey partridges *Perdix perdix. The Journal of Applied Ecology*, **33:** 965–978.

148 Lanz, M., Michler, S. & Duplain, J. (2012) *Projet de conservation de la perdrix grise Perdix perdix dans le canton de Genève. Rapport final de la phase de project 2007-2012.*

149 Bro, E., Mayot, P., Corda, E. & Reitz, F. (2004) Impact of habitat management on grey partridge populations: assessing wildlife cover using a multisite BACI experiment. *Journal of Applied Ecology*, **41:** 846–857.

150 Homberger, B., Duplain, J., Jenny, M. & Jenni, L. (2017) Agri-evironmental schemes and active nest protection can increase hatching success of a reintroduced farmland bird species. *Landscape and Urban Planning*, **161:** 44–51.

151 Knaus, P., Antoniazza, S., Wechsler, S., Guélat, J., Kéry, M., Sattler, N. & Strebel, T. (2018) *Schweizer Brutvogelatlas 2013-2016. Verbreitung und Bestandsentwicklung der Vögel in der Schweiz und im Fürstentum Lichtenstein.* Vogelwarte. Sempach.

152 Rickenbach, O., Grüebler, M.U., Schaub, M., Koller, A., Naef-Daenzer, B. & Schifferli, L. (2011) Exclusion of ground predators improves Northern Lapwing *Vanellus vanellus* chick survival. *Ibis*, **153**: 531–542.

153 Schifferli, L., Rickenbach, O., Koller, A. & Grüebler, M. (2009) Nest protection from agriculture and predation to improve nest and chick survival of the northern lapwing *Vanellus vanellus* in Swiss farmland. *Ornithologische Beobachter*, **106**: 311–326.

154 Malpas, L.R., Kennerley, R.J., Hirons, G.J.M., Sheldon, R.D., Ausden, M., Gilbert, J.C. & Smart, J. (2013) The use of predator-exclusion fencing as a management tool improves the breeding success of waders on lowland wet grassland. *Journal for Nature Conservation*, **21**: 37–47.

155 Zellweger-Fischer, J., Kéry, M. & Pasinelli, G. (2011) Population trends of brown hares in Switzerland: the role of land-use and ecological compensation areas. *Biological Conservation*, **144**: 1364–1373.

156 Holzgang, O., Heynen, D. & Kéry, M. (2005) Rückkehr des Feldhasen dank ökologischem Ausgleich? *Schriftenreihe der FAL*, **56**: 150–160.

157 Petrovan, S.O., Ward, A.I. & Wheeler, P.M. (2013) Habitat selection guiding agri-environment schemes for a farmland specialist, the brown hare. *Animal Conservation*, **16**: 344–352.

158 Draycott, R.A.H. (2012) Restoration of a sustainable wild grey partridge shoot in Eastern England. *Animal Biodiversity and Conservation*, **35**: 381–386.

159 Tapper, S.C., Green, R.E. & Rands, M.R.W. (1982) Effects of mammalian predators on partridge populations. *Mammal Review*, **12**: 159–167.

160 Ewald, J.A., Aebischer, N.J. & Brockless, M.H. (2009) Grey partridge recovery project: final update. *GWCT Annual Review*, **41**: 28–29.

161 Buner, F.D., Brockless, M.H. & Aebischer, N.J. (2016) The Rotherfield demonstration project. *The GWCT Annual Review*, **48**: 32–33.

162 IUCN/SSC. (2013) *Guidelines for Reintroductions and Other Conservation Translocations.* Gland, Switzerland.

163 IUCN/SSC & World Pheasant Association. (2009) *Guidelines for the Re-introduction of Galliformes for Conservation Purposes.* Gland, Switzerland and Newcastle-upon-Tyne, UK.

164 White, P.J.C., Stoate, C., Szczur, J. & Norris, K. (2014) Predator reduction with habitat management can improve songbird nest success. *Journal of Wildlife Management*, **78**: 402–412.

165 Bolton, M., Tyler, G., Smith, K. & Bamford, R. (2007) The impact of predator control on lapwing *Vanellus vanellus* breeding success on wet grassland nature reserves. *Journal of Applied Ecology*, **44**: 534–544.

166 Aebischer, N.J. (1991) Sustainable yields: gamebirds as a harvestable resource. In: *Proceedings of the International Conference 'Wise Use as a Conservation Strategy'; Gibier Faune Sauvage*: **8**: 335–351. (eds. Potts, G.R., Lecocq, Y., Swift, J. & Havet, P.) Office National de la Chasse. Paris.

167 Panek, M. (2019) Long-term changes in chick survival rate and brood size in the grey partridge *Perdix perdix* in Poland. *Bird Study*, **66/2**: 289–292.

168 Vogelwarte Sempach (2020) https://www.vogelwarte.ch/en/projects/population-trends/state-of-birds/grey-partridge-another-farmland-bird-has-disappeared

This edition has been made possible by the North Sea Region Interreg programme, the Edwin Bouw Foundation, Oakbank Game & Conservation and Kings Crops.

Written by
Jen Brewin, Game & Wildlife Conservation Trust, UK
Francis Buner, Game & Wildlife Conservation Trust, UK
Julie Ewald, Game & Wildlife Conservation Trust, UK

Edited by
Eckhard Gottschalk, University Göttingen, Germany
Jules Bos, BirdLife, Netherlands
Frans van Alebeek, BirdLife, Netherlands
Thomas Scheppers, Research Institute for Nature and Forest (INBO), Belgium
Kathleen Vanhuyse, Flemish Hunters Association, Belgium
David Parish, Game & Wildlife Conservation Trust, UK
Nicholas Aebischer, Game & Wildlife Conservation Trust, UK

Illustrations
Anne-Lieke Struijk-Faber, BirdLife, Netherlands

Graphic design
Saiid & Smale, Amsterdam. Alterations for English version: Chloe Stevens, Game & Wildlife Conservation Trust, UK

PARTRIDGE Steering committee members and supporters
United Kingdom: Natural England, NatureScot, Oakbank Game & Conservation, Kings Crops. **The Netherlands:** BoerenNatuur, Province Noord-Brabant. **Belgium:** Natuurpunt. **Germany:** Staatliche Vogelschutzwarte Niedersachsens, Deutscher Verband für Landschaftspflege, Deutsche Wildtier Stiftung, Deutscher Jagdverband, Manfred Hermsen Stiftung, Heinz Sielmann Stiftung, NABU. **France:** Association Nationale de Conservation du Petit Gibier. **International:** North Sea Region Interreg programme, Institute for European Environmental Policy (IEEP), European Landowners Organisation – Wildlife Estates Label (ELO), European Federation for Hunting and Conservation (FACE), International Association of Falconers (IAF).

ISBN number: 978-1-901369-38-0

Reference recommendation: Jen Brewin, Francis Buner and Julie Ewald (2020). *Farming with nature – promoting biodiversity across Europe through partridge conservation.* The Game & Wildlife Conservation Trust, Fordingbridge, UK